fantastic

WHEN BEING GOOD IS NOT ENOUGH

Alan Austin-Smith

CAPSTONE

For my beautiful wife Anny.
Anyone who knows her, knows that I'm the luckiest guy there is!

Cover design: Fantastic IP Ltd

© 2013 Alan Austin-Smith

Registered office
Capstone Publishing Ltd. (A Wiley Company), John Wiley and Sons Ltd, The Atrium, Southern Gate, Chichester, West Sussex, PO19 8SQ, United Kingdom

For details of our global editorial offices, for customer services and for information about how to apply for permission to reuse the copyright material in this book please see our website at www.wiley.com.

A catalogue record for this book is available from the British Library.

ISBN 978-0-857-08396-8 (paperback) ISBN 978-0-857-08430-9 (ebk)
ISBN 978-0-857-08431-6 (ebk) ISBN 978-0-857-08432-3 (ebk)

Text design by Deliverers Consultancy Ltd, London

Set in 9 on 11 pt Frutiger by Toppan Best-set Premedia Limited, Hong Kong

Printed in the United Kingdom by Bell & Bain Ltd, Glasgow

ACKNOW-LEDGEMENTS

Huge thanks to Dominic Sharpe for having the vision to support the 'fantastic' concept, the amazing team at Deliverers, particularly Matt, for making the book look so amazing and to Sarah Morgan – the way you pulled all the different elements together in the timescale that you had was incredible – thank you Sarah!

People always ask me how long it takes to write my books. The corny answer is a lifetime – but it's true! It's impossible to mention here all the 'fantastic' teachers, mentors and experiences that have influenced what I teach – but thank you.

Family is the most important thing in my life – my children, Craig, Sam and Nathan and my niece Shelly, you are all such beautiful people, it's impossible to put into words what I feel about you all – but I know that I could never achieve anything in my life that tops it.

My Hero! Tony Field

'People need People' – the words of a famous song. Tim, Sam, Nique, Fiona, Jenny, Nick Wood, Gaye, Angela, Niall and Anny – your unfailing support and belief has gone above and beyond. Myself and I want you to know that we have never and will never take for granted your commitment to the dream.

And finally, they say, behind every man... Well I have two! Anny, my beautiful wife and best friend – and Carolyn – my business partner (and amazing book editor!), wonderful friend, and ex wife!

Together, you are the shoulders I stand upon. What a journey! How long have we talked about this book?

Well, it's here now – let's enjoy it!!

Good is the new nice!!

Imagine you are somewhere listening in on a conversation about....YOU!

Two people are talking about you and they don't know that you can hear what they are saying.

One of them could be a customer of yours, your boss, a team mate, a friend maybe or a parent from your children's school, a past or present lover, whoever it was, wouldn't you want to listen in?

What if one of them didn't know you that well and they wanted to know more about you, as in – what you were like in; your job role/as a friend/parent/lover....? Now I know for certain you would be listening!!

The person who knows you replies; "um – they're... good."

You might think: "Huh? Is that it? Is that the best you can come up with?"

'Good' is now a bit ... average – a bit like nice!!

Do you want to be just 'good' at your job, or to be seen as being a 'nice' friend and can you imagine how it would feel to hear a lover describe your performance last night as just 'good'!!

I know I wouldn't be happy. I would have been hoping for something more like "They are Fantastic!!" Amazing! Brilliant! Incredible! Whichever word you want. I love Fantastic, but they all mean the same thing, simply...

Much better than good!!

Anybody can be good – in fact most people are. You don't hold on to a job for long if you aren't any good at what you do – but if you want more than survival, then you have to be more than good.

Good is not enough anymore!!

There's loads of 'good' around today but good is the new nice – it's average.

If we did some market research in any town 10 years ago on restaurants/hair salons/dentists/coffee shops etc., and we were looking for 'good' ones, the resulting graph would look something like this..

…with the few that were 'good' at the top of the graph and everyone else at different degrees down from the peak.

However, if we did that same research today I think the graph would look something like this...

…with a lot of places now registering as good.

Can you afford to just be 'good' – just the same as everyone else? No business or individual can afford that. To be successful you have to stand out – you have to get back to the peak again.

How? Be Fantastic! If we went searching for 'fantastic' restaurants etc., we would be back to the first graph. You have to differentiate yourself or your business and the way to do that today is to be FANTASTIC – not just good.

BE FANTASTIC –GOOD IS NOT ENOUGH ANY MORE!

FANTASTIC BIN MEN

I believe that to be fantastic at anything, you have to focus on what I call the other 50% – the 50% of what you do that makes the difference between good and fantastic.

I was having one of those strange conversations at a barbeque last year along the lines of 'Bin men ain't what they used to be!'. One woman interrupted though, saying that her bin men were fantastic (yes, she even used that word). What did she mean? Was she marvelling at the way they picked up her bags of rubbish and threw them in the back of the truck? I don't think so. I think she was talking about the fact that they smiled, said good morning, closed the gate etc.

On another occasion, I was due to do a coaching session with three surgeons. I must admit I did have some fears about what on earth I was going to do with them but a visit I made to an elderly relative in hospital a few weeks just before the session, gave me confidence.

When I asked my aunt how she was doing and if she was being looked after, she said "Oh yes. Everybody's been lovely and my surgeon is fantastic." (that word again).

Again – what was she talking about? Had they let her sit up and watch? Was it the skill and dexterity of the surgeon she was commenting on, how efficient they were? – Of course not. That, we would expect. No, she was telling me about how friendly they had been, how caring and understanding.

She was having a routine operation but as a 78-year-old who had never had an operation before, she was understandably very apprehensive. You can imagine can't you, that some surgeons would be very dismissive of her fears – just telling her not to worry – that it was just routine. Not this surgeon. This one understood her fears and spent time reassuring her, caring about her as a human being, chatting about her family etc., – she wasn't just seen as the 'next patient!'

It doesn't matter what you do, be it bin man, surgeon… the 50% rule applies.

50% of what makes you fantastic at what you do, is the other stuff...

Communication, attitude, confidence, motivation, self-management etc. It's this other stuff that enables you to do the things you have to do in your job or life and do them well.

Every sales person knows how to sell, but it's only the best ones that use the other stuff to achieve fantastic results. Every waiter or waitress knows how to smile, but...!

Studying fantastic people – successful people in all walks of life over a 25-year period – it is clear to me that they share common characteristics that apply to anyone.

It doesn't matter what it is you want to be fantastic at – 50% of it will be about these common factors – I call them the 7 characteristics of Fantastic People – the other 50%.

The Fantastic Revolution

Why is it a revolution? Because evolution is too slow today, the world is moving too fast. If you want to stay ahead, you have to be changing, learning and moving just as fast.

Surely anyone who says 'I'm already fantastic, I don't need to do anymore' – isn't!

That's really what this book is about – understanding how those 7 characteristics work and how you can use them yourself in all areas of your life, not just at work.

FANTASTIC PEOPLE ARE:
PASSIONATE
CREATIVE
DELIGHTING
PEOPLE
PERFORMERS
ALIVE INSIDE
ALWAYS
LEARNING
HAVING FUN

WHAT'S INSIDE

*BE
FANTASTIC
–GOOD
IS NOT
ENOUGH
ANY
MORE!*

When I wrote my first books, 'The Fantastic Hairdresser' and 'The Fantastic Boss', I wanted to create a different type of reading experience.

"I know I should read more, but..."

I have heard this comment so many times having been involved in sales, management and personal development training for over 25 years now. There are many reasons why people don't read as much as they should do, such as time etc., (we will deal with this later). However, I do feel that in a world that is changing so rapidly, there doesn't always seem to be much creativity and thought being put into the way a book is presented.

So, we looked at what people do read – the people who 'don't read as much as they should'.

Answer - magazines.

When we looked at how someone reads a magazine, they very rarely read it from cover to cover. They skim it first, then find a bit that appeals and read that, before putting it down and going back to it later to read another bit.

A magazine entices you to read it, with colour, visuals, different print styles and layout etc. You write in a magazine, fill out questionnaires and so on.

So, without turning it into a magazine, we created a different style of book that gives people the flexibility to use it as they wish.

If you are going to read 'Fantastic' from cover to cover, then I still suggest that you break it into small chunks. If you read this book in one sitting, you don't get the time to reflect on what you may have learnt and how it will affect you.

However, you can also use my books randomly – like a magazine – identifying bits that you like the sound of or that particularly relate to you and dip in and out as you wish. If you do decide to use it like this though, I would strongly suggest that you still read the first two chapters.

These introduce some core concepts that will give you the foundations of success and make everything else more relevant. After that, do as you wish. You will find ACTION pages at the end of each chapter. Of course it's up to you – I know it doesn't appeal to everybody, but I really would suggest that you use these pages to reflect on what you have learnt and identify areas that you want to take action on. It will increase the effectiveness of the book dramatically.

Be confident to write in this book, make it yours. Jot your thoughts and comments in the margin.

This is not just a book you read and then put on a shelf to gather dust.

It's a bit more like a handbook that you might keep in your bag and as such, you will probably want to go back to certain sections and review them. You may use it to coach others, to help people stretch themselves and realise their potential. So, add to this book, make it yours, add your own opinions, ideas and things you want to change. In fact, start right now and put your name in the front. Make it yours!

I love the fact that eventually every book out there becomes individual, unique, and different from the next one because of the personal views, opinions and pointers that you have added to it.

Finally, please recognise that this book is about being fantastic at what you do – whether that's at work or life in general. However, the emphasis must be on 'being' fantastic. We can all read books like this and talk a great story but nothing will change, nothing will happen unless we actually take action.

Don't just read about fantastic – BE IT!!

BE FANTASTIC IN AN INSTANT – THE INSTANT YOU DECIDE TO BE FANTASTIC RATHER THAN JUST 'GOOD' YOU ARE ACTUALLY 'BEING' FANTASTIC – NOW ALL YOU HAVE TO DO IS KEEP IT GOING!!

1

SUCCESS
WHAT IS IT?

Look at a clock or a watch – or if you can't find either, just count it. But I want you to remind yourself how long a second is. 1... 2. That's it, just one second. The difference between first and last place in the Olympic 100 metres final will be less than that – less than one second. The difference between first and second, will be measured in hundredths' of a second. Take that second again – 1... 2, and now break it down into hundredths and think about what one or two hundredths of a second is. You can't? Of course you can't. It is impossible to imagine but that can be the difference between success and failure.

What am I saying here? Simply, if the only difference between those eight athletes is less than 1 second, then they all have the technique, power and ability to run as fast as each other. So how come one or two of them will consistently win every time?

Successful people have always fascinated me.

Why does one athlete consistently win the 100 metres? Why does one footballer score more goals than another, a waitress get more tips, or a sales person hit more targets? Why does one manager consistently get fantastic results with a loyal team who are enjoying what they do?

They understand the 50% rule.

All sportspeople know how to play their sport and all the top ones know how to play it well, so what is the difference that makes champions? The other stuff! The 50% that is about attitude, confidence, motivation, communication etc. This isn't just true of sportspeople though – it applies to all of us in whatever we do. There are so many things we can learn from people who are achieving great things.

Successful people aren't more intelligent, they don't have bigger brains, they don't start with more money, and they all know how to do the 50%, that is what they do – it's the 'other stuff' that makes the difference.

Essentially we all have the same opportunities. You may kid yourself that you are a special case, but there are countless stories of people from disadvantaged backgrounds or who are not fully able in some way, that have achieved exceptional levels of success.

What is success?

This question is asked over and over again. It is often the cause of a lot of frustration and dissatisfaction as people spend their lives chasing something that isn't necessarily what they want.

Everybody wants to be successful, fantastic at what they do, don't they?

Well interestingly, some people tell me that they don't. It took me a while to work this out before I realised that all it was, the only difference, was people's perception of success. The people who say that they don't want to be successful are basing their understanding of success on one thing – what we are fed by the media etc.; money, cars, big promotions and so on.

Success isn't just about the material rewards, job title, or how many air miles you rack up – it's about being happy with what you are doing. Surely you want to enjoy what you do. I find it scary when I see those surveys that say how many people are not happy at work. It's crazy. It's such a major part of our life. Isn't it about time we did something about this?

It's not about mountain hopping though. When the going gets tough, too many people jump off the mountain onto what looks like an easier climb, but even that one will get tough at some point. Then they jump again – hopping from one mountain to another and never reaching the summit of any of them.

What we have to do if we want to be more successful is to stop looking for the easy option.

Stop blaming everybody and everything else for our seeming lack of success and take responsibility for changing the way we think and operate.

Start being brave enough to stand out – to be fantastic.

EVERYBODY WANTS TO BE SUCCESSFUL, FANTASTIC AT WHAT THEY DO, DON'T THEY?

Success is all about reward

Some people want the material rewards, of course, but to others, success is being a good parent, a fun friend, enjoying their job, regardless of how much money they have, or how big their house is.

So, who is right? Both are, because success is simply getting the rewards you want and then enjoying them. It is your life after all and as long as what you want is ethical, moral and legal who am I or anyone else for that matter, to judge you?

There are four types of reward in general:

Community Reward – The reward people get from helping other people – this is not just the obvious – care workers, nurses, charity workers and similar people, it's people who get a kick out of other people's happiness and enjoyment. Some of the best customer service performers get their satisfaction this way.

Personal Reward – This is when the reward comes from your own personal satisfaction in what you have achieved.

Security Reward – People who are motivated by this reward often think that they do not have a passion for success, sometimes saying things like;

"As long as I can pay my bills, go on holiday and have a reasonable standard of living – I'm happy – I don't need fancy cars etc."

However, what if you can't pay your bills, have a holiday etc? Then you are not achieving the success you want – you still want to be successful but it's just your version of success.

Material Reward – This is the one that most people associate with 'success'. If material rewards turn you on – great! If they don't though, it doesn't mean you don't want to be successful, you are just looking for different rewards.

Community reward	
Personal reward	
Security reward	
Material reward	

Put the four rewards in order of preference for yourself – remember there is no right or wrong answer – most people want a bit of all of them, but it's important to identify which ones motivate you the most so that you can focus on getting the rewards you want.

START BEING BRAVE ENOUGH TO STAND OUT - TO BE FANTASTIC

A successful life is made up of millions of moments

Let's take this a stage further. We are talking about success and I guess we all want to have a successful life.

Do you want to be eternally happy? Be successful in your life?

Well, let me show you how.

The problem is that a lot of people don't really understand what 'life' is. So, how can you have a successful one, if you don't even know what it is?

To be happy in your life, you have to understand what life is.

Let me ask you a couple of questions, strange as they may seem: Can I kill you now, right now this moment – yesterday? Can I kill you now, right now – tomorrow? Of course I can't – you are not alive yet tomorrow. And you are not alive yesterday anymore either. So when can I kill you? NOW, is the answer. The only time I could take your life is now, because it's the only moment it is there to be taken!

You may not have thought about it like this before, but there is only one moment you are alive – when your heart is beating, your mind is thinking and your body is breathing – and that moment is NOW.

So, what is life? It's now – it is happening right now as you read these words.

We need to stop looking at life as a whole – a 70 to 80 year long experience. Life is made up of millions of moments. Every life is made up of so many years, each year is made up of 365 days and every day is filled with many moments.

Moments of love, fun, energy, achievement, excitement, satisfaction, or simply the accomplishment of some task in your work or life.

I know what some of you are thinking though:

"What about the crappy moments; the moments of despair, disappointment, lost love, anger, tiredness, boredom and failure?"

We will come to those in a moment, but for now let's just work on the premise that they are all moments, whether they are good or bad.

THE PAST AND THE FUTURE

If life is made up of millions of moments, the only control you have in your life is in the current one. Think about it:

What can you do about the past?

Only one thing – learn from it. Learn how to have a good time – you have good pasts and you can learn how not to have a bad time from the not so good ones. But that is it!

EVERY DAY IS FILLED WITH MILLIONS OF MOMENTS

Once you have learnt the lessons, there is nothing else you can do about the past. You can't change it, it has happened. Makes you wonder why we spend so much time beating ourselves up for the mistakes we have made in the past. Once you have learned from them – that's it, there is nothing you can do to change them.

What about the future, what can we do about that?

Plan for it, prepare for it, dream about it, but that's all – you don't even know if it's going to happen. What do personal, or world disasters teach us? What does a near miss in the car teach us, or a health scare? That life is fragile; none of us have a clue what is going to happen in the next five minutes, let alone five years.

How many plans have changed in your life? Some for the better, some for the worse but I bet there are plenty. Now think about how much time and energy we waste worrying about what might happen in the future – a future that we know we have no control over. Crazy, isn't it?

TAKE CONTROL

A successful life is a life filled with lots of little successes.

Take control – the way you deal with each moment in your life, determines how successful it is. The more successful, happy moments you have, the happier and more successful you will be.

So, what about those crappy moments I promised we would deal with? Well, they will always be there

We are human beings and all have negative emotions and issues to deal with but, when we realise that these are still just moments – moments that pass – that become a history for us to learn from, they are much easier to deal with.

The more we understand this, the easier it is to move past the genuinely bad times. But also to change the way we are operating or thinking at those times and turn some of the crappy moments into better ones.

Movie libraries

I call these moments 'movies' – we all have two movie libraries in our heads – one which holds the video nasties – all the failures in your life, the embarrassments, bad experiences, loves you have lost, things you can't do, people who intimidate you, etc.

The first thing to understand is that everybody – and I mean everybody – has these movies in their life. However, people who appear to be having a more successful, happy life are simply spending time watching the movies in the other library...

The Sunday afternoon movies! The success you have achieved, (remember what your definition of success is) the great times, the people who love you, the things you do well, etc.

On our seminars, we do an exercise that helps people realise that they sometimes don't spend enough time watching the right movies.

I ask the audience to think of three successful moments in their life, write them on a post-it® note and stick them up on the wall.

It doesn't have to be some huge world changing success – it could simply be passing your driving test or receiving praise for something you did at school, home or work. I can still vividly remember scoring the winning goal in our football team's cup final when I was 8!

Then I ask the audience to do the same with happy moments, really good memories. Some of the moments are really different, ranging from laughing with a friend through to swimming with dolphins or something as simple as being greeted by your dog at the front gate. Some of the moments are far too rude for me to divulge, but I'm sure you can use your imagination!

It's a fantastic exercise. Everyone in the room thinking of happy and successful moments from their past, writing them down and sticking them proudly on the wall. I then ask them to do it again – think of another three... And again. The interesting thing is, it starts to get easier as you get into the groove of thinking about those things. It makes you realise that we don't spend enough time recognising the good stuff that has happened in our lives, often focusing too much on the crappy stuff.

Try it for yourself. Fill in the post-it® notes to the right or visit the 'millions of moments' page on the website and post them there. You will see other people's moments there – they will remind you of loads that you have forgotten – I promise!

3 Happy Moments

3 Successful Moments

3 More Happy Moments

TOTAL LIFE CONCEPT

Live on the edge

This wonderful tool started life as the Total Product Concept, a marketing tool that I learnt from Tom Peters. However, the more I used it, the more I realised that it wasn't just about marketing or even business. It was about everything.

That's why I named it TLC – the

Total Life Concept:

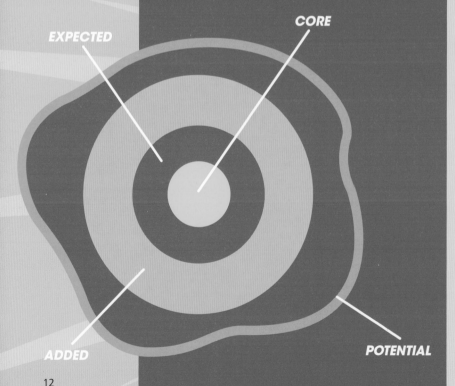

EXPECTED

CORE

ADDED

POTENTIAL

The Core

It starts at the centre with the core being what you do. For example, the core reason a hotel exists is – people need a bed when they are away from their own. A coffee shop exists so that people can buy coffee and restaurants are for eating in.

The Expected

Then it moves out to the next ring, with 'expected'. I go to a hotel to sleep in a bed but I expect a bathroom and a certain level of cleanliness and hygiene. I expect a certain level of service in a coffee shop, I expect a certain ambience and atmosphere in the restaurant – it's not the only reason why I go there – the core – but it's what I expect when I get there.

How many people do you know that stop here, doing what's expected and no more? For instance, the person who finishes work on the dot, regardless of what needs to be done. The receptionist who won't answer the phone on their break or the salesperson who only ever 'just' achieves their targets – they have all stopped in 'expected'.

I was discussing business training once with a restaurant owner, who came out with a line I will always remember. He didn't see that he needed any training as in his own words:

"We are no worse than anyone else in this town!"

Isn't that amazing? I am a very visual person and I already had a whole marketing campaign going on in my mind – posters at key sites, banners in the window, newspaper adverts all carrying the line: "Come to us, we are no worse than anyone else!" If anything sums up people stopping at 'expected' then that line is it.

The Added

The next ring is the 'added' part of the model. Going further than expected, taking that extra step, exceeding the expectations. We all know what this feels like when it happens to us. It's great.

"I expected a certain level of service – but wow, I didn't expect this!"

YOU HAVE TO BE ON THE EDGE – CHANGING, LEARNING AND INNOVATING ALL OF THE TIME

When any individual or company goes beyond expectations, they create a fantastic response.

I know a beauty therapist who sends 'thank you' cards to all her new clients! It is not the company policy, she does it off her own back.

When I discovered this person, she was working in a new salon with three other therapists. Six months down the line, only one of the four is consistently fully booked. No prize for guessing which one!

Is this where the winners are?

Well, it certainly looks like it, but actually it's not. In fact, if you are sitting in 'added', patting yourself on the back for all the great things that you do – you are actually in 'expected' and you probably don't even realise it.

The Potential

It is this final part of the Total Life Concept where you find the winners. 'Potential'. It's here where you ask: "What's next? Now what do I do?"

It's here where you find the key to survival in this ever-changing world – Creativity.

As I have just said, many people are sitting around in 'added' feeling good about themselves because of what they do and how they do it. Not realising that what was once special – the service your company provides, the way you manage your team, run meetings, praise people, achieve targets, the marketing you do, has become the norm – expected.

The only way to stay ahead is to be constantly in 'potential'. Always moving, growing and learning – creatively looking for what's next.

The story of a kettle

You see, the model works from the outside in. A hotel somewhere, whilst in 'potential' (the outside) – decided to put kettles in all of their rooms. The moment they did this, the kettle moved into the 'added' part of the model and you as the guest, were pleasantly surprised to find a kettle in your room.

But now, if you checked into a hotel tonight – you would 'expect' a kettle in your room.

So the kettle in a hotel room started its life in 'potential', moved into 'added' and finished up in 'expected'.

This happens to everything!

Think about it and you will see I'm right. Everything starts with a creative idea, spends a period of time being unique, different, special, before eventually becoming the norm and ending up as expected. If you are not in 'potential', you are in 'expected' – standing still in the one place you can't afford to if you want to be successful today.

The challenge today for any individual or business is that the time spent in the 'added' part of the model – the 'WOW' – is getting shorter and shorter due to the speed of change in the world around us.

Remember, it's not that long ago that a phone with a camera was unique and, who gets excited anymore when you see a smart phone, or computer tablet? They are all WOW things that are becoming the 'norm' really quickly.

THAT'S WHY BEING ON THE EDGE – IN POTENTIAL – IS SO CRITICAL, AS IT'S THE ONLY WAY YOU CAN CONSISTENTLY BE IN 'ADDED' – *DOING MORE THAN IS EXPECTED OF YOU*

SUCCESS IS ABOUT REWARD

Success is different for all of us – it's about the rewards we get from what we do and we all want different rewards – however, we all want the reward – we all want to be 'successful' whatever that word means to you!

A SUCCESSFUL LIFE IS MADE UP OF MILLIONS OF MOMENTS

Every life will have different moments – millions of moments – some will be fantastic moments and some won't – it's called 'life'!

A moment that isn't great is just that – a moment! Are you focusing on the moments that are fantastic in your life or the ones that aren't?

Success is your choice!

LIVE ON THE EDGE

We live in a fast changing world whether you like it or not – the only way to stay ahead of it in every area of your life is to understand the 'Total Life Concept'.

You have to be on the edge – changing, learning and innovating all of the time.

Choose 3 goals from this chapter that you can take immediate action on:

1

2

3

2

LEARN FROM FANTASTIC PEOPLE

You can't learn to be successful!

This is a model that I created after spending many years studying fantastic people in all walks of life.

Success is at the peak of the pyramid, which is obviously where we are going, but I want to start in the centre with – learn.

The first lesson I discovered is simply that you can't learn to be successful.

Everybody is trying it, reading books, magazines, going on courses, surfing the internet. There's no question many people are committed to learning today but I fear that some, in their last moments of this life, will be saying: "I did all that learning but nothing ever happened for me. Nothing changed."

You can't just learn to be successful.

Learning on its own will not take you to success.

It's the word above it in the pyramid that makes the difference.

ACTION

The population can quite easily be split into those who are taking the action they need to and those who are waiting for it to happen to them.

SUCCESS

ACT

LEARN

DISCIPLINE

RESPONSIBILITY

THE MILLIONAIRE HAIRDRESSER

This true story is a great example of the pyramid in action.

A hairdresser I know, was just 21 years old when she learnt a tool from me called the 10% rule. Simply, it means saving 10% of your salary to invest in your future.

She was only earning around £150 per week at the time but still managed to put **£15** a week away. She also decided to add half her tips to that as well, which was another **£15** a week – giving her a total of £120 per month equating to **£1,440** per year.

She then realised that if she could increase her sales, it meant she could add as much as £50 per week to her wages, which gave her another **£5** a week to add to her savings – an extra **£240** per year giving her **£1,680** that year.

The next year she decided to put 20% away. She was now earning £250 per week with about £40 a week in tips. The 20% added to half her tips gave her **£70** a week to put away – **£3,360** by the end of the year.

She now had **£5,040** saved! She used this as a deposit on a small flat for herself worth **£50,000**. That was 15 years ago.

That flat is now worth **£150,000** and she only has 10 years left on the mortgage.

Here is the really interesting bit though – she carried on putting her 20% aside. Her salary grew, as did her tips – and two years later, she bought another flat which she rented out whilst living in her original flat.

She has just purchased her 7th property – having bought one every two years for the last 14 years.

She is now a 36-year-old stylist – she decided she didn't want her own salon, or even any management responsibility, she just loves doing her job.

She also has a property portfolio currently worth over £1,700,000.

This is a hairdresser – not a business owner, not an industry icon – just a normal stylist who did something special.

However, even though it was special, it was something that anyone can do.

Some people misunderstand this story, saying that she was just lucky to hit the property market at the right time. That's not the point. The point is,

she took action on something she'd learnt!

That's it – that's all she did. But to do it, she needed the other parts of the pyramid – responsibility and discipline.

Firstly, she had to take responsibility to listen to me, as I hope you are now, and think, "that's me, I need to get more control over my money. It's up to me." Then she had to have the discipline to keep it going, to stay focused on why she was doing what she was doing.

Interestingly, she will tell you that eventually this became easy because it became a habit – a part of her life. So discipline was not a problem any more.

SHE HAS JUST PURCHASED HER *7TH PROPERTY* – HAVING BOUGHT ONE EVERY TWO YEARS FOR THE LAST 14 YEARS

23

If it's to be - it's up to me

This is such a cliché - I normally try and avoid the more obvious ones but this one is so true it has made its way into the book.

There are so many people who are not achieving what they want and have every excuse or reason under the sun why. But how many times do we feel humbled by people who are starting off with less than us, or with greater challenges than we have, but are still achieving great things.

To be fantastic, we have to start looking at ourselves. It's the foundation of the success pyramid – take responsibility.

It is important that you understand the difference between responsibility and blame, or fault. Of course sometimes you are taking responsibility for the blame – "it was my fault." But there is a difference between the two.

Many people say to me that their 'boss' doesn't respect them, doesn't communicate well, or doesn't have any time for them. Or I hear that their partner in life doesn't give them the love and affection that they would like.

Often these people are saying it's not my fault. Maybe it isn't but my question is always the same: "Do you want it to change?" If the answer is yes, then it is your responsibility to do something about it, even if it's not your fault.

*If you want change,
change something.*

The fly test

Picture a sunny day. You're in the kitchen and the back door is open. A fly flies into your kitchen and as it buzzes around, it sees through the window – blue sky, trees and grass. That's what I'm looking for it thinks, and heads straight for it.

Now you may be surprised to know that flies have no perception of glass! SMACK! It must be quite a shock. However, the fly seems to recover quite well and continues buzzing around until again, it sees through the window – blue sky, trees and grass and SMACK! They don't learn too well these flies. In fact it will carry on doing this for hours if you let it.

The fly keeps repeating the behaviour that is getting it nowhere. If only it would just go in a different direction, it would achieve the desired result – the back door is open!

So that's the fly test –

repeating a behaviour that is getting us nowhere, over and over and over again.

We all need to take a fly test sometimes in our life.

How many people do you know that want changes in their life but are not prepared to change anything?

People who want to stop smoking, but continue to put cigarettes in their mouth. People who want to lose weight, but continue to eat too much. People who want to get fit, but don't go to the gym. People who want to save money, but continue to spend more than they earn.

If you want change, change something.

Fantastic people understand that they have to take responsibility.

There are people standing beside the road of life with their thumb out waiting to be taken to where they want to go, whilst others are already driving there.

SUCCESS

THE 7 CHARACTERISTICS OF FANTASTIC PEOPLE

THE FANTASTIC REVOLUTION

Ok, let's get Fantastic!

As I have already mentioned, I spend a lot of time researching, learning from and listening to fantastic people in all walks of life. From the high performers in business, sport or entertainment, world leaders and influencers to the amazing wealth of learning from 'normal' people in everyday life that are just simply fantastic at their jobs, their relationships, helping and caring for others, dealing with adversity etc.

From all that learning, the common factors which shaped the Fantastic Revolution started to become clear.

The order of the characteristics is not so much an order of preference, but more an order of logic – that each one empowers the next and so on.

Fantastic people are passionate

It starts with Passion – Fantastic people are passionate about what they are doing, actually to be more accurate – they are passionate about why they are doing what they are doing.

Fantastic people are creative

Fantastic people understand that today's 'wow' will quickly become tomorrow's 'norm'. Therefore fantastic people are creative – understanding the need for constant re-invention, innovation and change.

Fantastic people delight

Fantastic people understand they can't do it all on their own – they need happy customers, they need a committed team, great relationships, business or financial support, etc.

Richard Branson is a great example of this – he has always understood that he needs great people alongside him. Fantastic people need to enchant people, to inspire them – they need to delight their customers, friends, family, business associates and teammates.

Fantastic people are performers

Life is a stage – and we are all performers on that stage – do you want to be the lead or part of the chorus? Actually, as we have already discussed, there is nothing wrong with being in the chorus if that is what you want. However, you are on stage, either way, you still have to perform! Confidence is such a critical factor in having fun in your life yet so many people are held back by a lack of confidence – learn to be a performer and get control of any fears that may be stopping you from being fantastic.

Fantastic people are alive on the inside

If you are going to be alive on the outside – passionate, creative, delighting people and performing – then you have to be alive on the inside. Fantastic people understand that (what I call) 'external motivation' (motivation from other people or external sources) is just the icing on the cake. It is the 'internal motivation' we have to rely on, simply because we have absolute control over it, we are not waiting to be motivated – we do it ourselves. That's what I call being alive on the inside!

Fantastic people are always learning

I guess you wouldn't have got this far in the book if you didn't agree with this one. Fantastic people are always learning. 'Jack of all trades' used to be a negative reference – in today's world it is almost essential – if you aren't constantly learning new things, keeping up with the pace of this crazy world we live in, you will be left behind so rapidly it can become almost impossible to catch up.

Fantastic people are having fun

Finally, the 7th characteristic is possibly the most important one as it completes the cycle, enabling you to keep on going. Because if you aren't having fun it will be very difficult to keep the passion that fuels the creativity, which generates the ideas that you will delight people with. Delighting people needs a performance from you, which means you have to be motivated to learn new things and to keep on having fun – which will keep the passion that fuels the creativity...!

The Fantastic Revolution really is a revolution. When you look at the 7 characteristics this way, it is easy to see how it works:

Passion

Being passionate about what you want to achieve and why you want to achieve it.

Create

Then you have to be creative in how you are going to achieve it.

Delight

You will need help – you need customers to love you, colleagues and partners to be committed and support from family and friends.

Performer

Now it's time for action – you will need the confidence to take the action required.

Alive Inside

But you have to keep taking that action – you will have to be self-motivated to keep the discipline needed.

Always Learning

You have to be learning all the time as everything will have changed in a short time.

Fun

And finally, you have to enjoy it, otherwise you will never make it happen. That enjoyment fuels the passion – which loops us around to begin the revolution again.

Being Fantastic is self-perpetuating when you get it right!

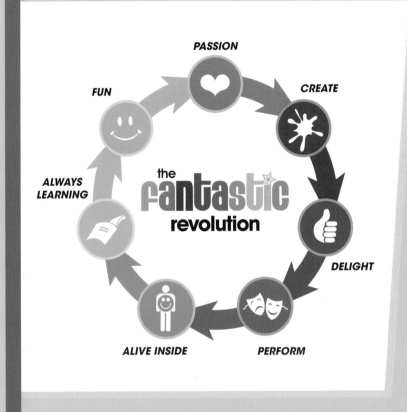

YOU CAN'T LEARN TO BE SUCCESSFUL!

It doesn't matter how much you learn about success, nothing will happen unless you take action and then have the self-discipline and perseverance to keep taking action. What's the point of doing all that learning and then never taking action?

IF YOU WANT CHANGE, CHANGE SOMETHING

Fantastic people understand they need to take responsibility. If you want things to be different – you need to do something different – it's no good just wishing for things to change whilst you carry on doing the same stuff that isn't working for you!

THE FLY TEST

Everybody needs to take the 'fly test' in different areas of their life. What behaviours are you repeating over and over again which are getting you nowhere?

Like a fly trying to get out of a closed window – change direction and you might find the door is open behind you!

Choose 3 goals from this chapter that you can take immediate action on:

1

2

3

3

FANTASTIC PEOPLE ARE PASSIONATE

Fantastic people are in love!

I ask the same question of every 'fantastic' person I ever interview:

"Why are you fantastic at what you do?"

Once we get through the modesty and humility that so many of these people have and I persuade them that they are 'fantastic' at what they do, the answer is always along the lines of;

"I love it – I love what I do."

Of all the characteristics, passion is the most common of all as it is shared by everybody who is fantastic at what they do, and perhaps most interestingly is always absent from those who are not!

I think most of us start something with a passion – a new job, a relationship, a hobby, even things like a diet, fitness class etc.

It's when we lose the passion that things go wrong – we begin to hate our job, fall out of love, give up our new hobby or stop going to the gym.

Why does this happen? It isn't about whether we are passionate about what we do – it is about why we lose the passion. If we can solve that one then we will know how to get it back again.

The more I thought about it the more I realised that passion is all about focus.

Where you put your focus is where you get your results!

I have always believed that where you put your focus is where you get your results. My favourite example which everybody seems to be able to relate to is when you are looking to buy a new car. You decide which one you like and then what happens? You see it everywhere.

It is simply the way our brain operates – there is a filter in our brain that sorts out the relevant things from the mass of information that our senses are being bombarded with, in any one moment.

The human eye can distinguish one photon of light. Our nose can identify one molecule of smell. So much of this is happening at an unconscious level where we are completely unaware of it. With this level of information entering the brain constantly, we need to have some sort of filter system, which decides what our conscious mind needs to be aware of. Otherwise we would all go insane from the overload.

This filter is what makes focus so important. When you focus on something, you are giving the filter in your brain the information that will help it sort through the mass. That's why you start seeing those cars all of a sudden – they were always there, it's just you hadn't previously given your filter the focus it needed to notice them.

Assuming you accept this principle – let's look at the flip side to it. If you accept that where you put your focus is where you get your results – what happens if you put your focus in the wrong place?

You get the wrong results!

WHEN YOU FOCUS ON SOMETHING, **YOU ARE GIVING THE FILTER IN YOUR BRAIN THE INFORMATION THAT WILL HELP IT SORT THROUGH THE MASS**

WHY DO YOU DO WHAT YOU DO?

Understand the difference between 'what' you do every day and 'why' you do it.

Imagine you met me at a party and asked me what I do? I wouldn't – but I could answer like this.

"I drive up and down motorways – sit in traffic jams, stand in queues at airport security, spend time away from my family in lonely hotel rooms that all look the same, stand in conference rooms that are often too small, too big, too warm, too cold and talk to people – some of whom don't even want to listen to me, make phone calls, send e-mails..."

Of course you wouldn't let me get that far – you would interrupt and say "No – what's your job?"

"Oh, my job, sorry, you asked me what I do!"

I am very clear about what my job is – my job is to communicate to people in such a way as to motivate them to fly – to be fantastic. I love my job, but of course I don't always love some of the things I have to do!

I really don't enjoy queuing in airports, taking half my clothes off to get through security and then finding out that my flight has been delayed – but if that is what I have to do, to do what I love – then I can do it!

The passion comes from why you do things – not just what you do – of course we are passionate about some of the things that we do, however we all have things that we don't enjoy doing.

Let's face it – who can honestly say they like changing a nappy? But you will happily do it because of the reason why you do it – the happiness and comfort of your child!

*Focus on the crap
and you get...Crap!*

You have probably experienced this with some of the relationships in your life. We have all experienced a time when for some reason all we could see about another person was the stuff that annoyed us. Often, it's small silly insignificant stuff, but it is all we are focused on. It affects everything you feel about that person – negatively.

What would happen if you were to re-focus? Think about all the things you love or like about that person, their strengths rather than their weaknesses.

I guarantee that you will begin to feel differently about that person.

Well, it's the same with your job. If you have fallen into the trap of only seeing what is wrong with your job, the negative elements – and trust me, there is no such job that doesn't have those elements – then that is all you will see.

Dancing street cleaners

It is a short step from this to hating your job. Becoming miserable and depressed by it, not wanting to go to work. Of course that will affect the way you operate at work so you will not be as successful, maybe not earn as much money, not have the respect from your colleagues or bosses – then wow, are you on a downward spiral.

Do you know what will happen then? You will leave, or get fired, get a new job with all the excitement that you had at the beginning in your previous job. But eventually you will start to feel the same, and the cycle will start all over again.

Some people spend their whole working life like this, and do you know who they blame? Everybody and everything else!

There are people doing what would generally be perceived as not being a great job – but some of them choose to enjoy it – to have fun doing it.

There are two types of street cleaner – one who thinks they spend their day picking up other people's rubbish or the one who understands that they are helping to make their community a nicer and safer place. When you know 'why' you are doing something, you can be a street cleaner who dances while they clean!

The next time you feel like you have lost passion – press the pause button and ask yourself where your focus is – I guarantee that you will find yourself focusing on the crap! Where you put your focus...! Focus on the crap and you will get crap results – shift your focus to the things you enjoy doing and the reasons why you do them and the passion will come back!

Where are you going?

So, passion is about focus. Goals, objectives, dreams, targets – call it whatever you like – it all means the same thing – having some sort of idea of where you are going and why.

If you have children, you have probably sat and read the classic stories to them – the ones you read yourself when you were a child. Did you notice how they often read differently as an adult, to how they did as a child?

My favourite children's classic to read as an adult, is Lewis Carroll's – Alice in Wonderland. There are so many metaphors it is almost a personal development book. Like when Alice meets the Cheshire cat:

"Would you tell me please," says Alice, "which way I ought to go from here?" "Well that depends a good deal on where you want to get to." said the cat.

"Oh I don't much care where." said Alice. "Then it doesn't matter which way you go." said the cat.

So many people are like Alice, not knowing where they are going, or why they are going there – just on a journey to somewhere, hoping that where they end up will be where they want to be!

Where are you going exactly?

Imagine you were a passenger in a car and asked the driver: "Where are we going?" They reply: "I don't know. We are just going to drive around and hopefully we will end up somewhere nice!"

That's the first level of focus – none at all!!

People say to me: "Oh I do know where I am going, what I want. I definitely want to be more successful, make more money, be happy, have a good standard of living etc."

This is the second level of focus and is almost as bad as not having a clue where you are going – if we were back in the car again the answer would be: "We are going north." – You still don't know where you are going really, you can't plan the journey or work out what you have to do to get there.

It is only when the driver knows exactly where they are going that you can get the map out and work out how to get there, how long it will take, what provisions you might need etc., etc.

How can you expect to get 'there' if you don't know where 'there' is. How can you be motivated to achieve something if you don't know what that something is?

KNOW WHERE YOU ARE GOING - *EXACTLY!*

Remember the why

If we stick to the same analogy and you told me exactly where we were going – I would still want to know why we were going there?

I once asked a very wealthy man who had made and lost a fortune twice previously – how he had managed to keep his fortune this time. His answer was enlightening: "I knew WHY I wanted the money this time. Previously I just wanted to be rich. This time I was clear about what I wanted to achieve with the money."

He knew where he was going, but he also knew why he was going there!

Be excited about where you are going

Your where and why have to excite you.

We are talking about passion here remember!

Do you want to achieve certain things in your job or do you want to buy a property; get a new car; take up a new hobby/interest?

Maybe you have a passion for something – are you concerned for the environment, supporting the elderly or committed to humanitarian aid?

There is no right or wrong – it's simply whatever it is that turns you on!

Your 'why' might not even have anything to do with what you are doing currently – maybe you are doing a job that allows you to achieve a 'why' that has nothing to do with your job. This 'why' though is still the reason that you need to be passionate about being fantastic at your job.

An actor who is waiting tables whilst waiting for their big break still needs to be a fantastic waiter/waitress, otherwise they might lose their job, or miss an opportunity to be noticed by an agent etc.

I know a postman who does what he does so that he can have the afternoon to do something he is passionate about. However he understands that he has to be a fantastic postman to make sure he keeps the job that gives him the freedom to do that.

Knowing where you are going and why you are going there is what gives you the passion to be fantastic at what you do – whatever it is.

KEEP THE PASSION BY KNOWING WHERE YOU *ARE GOING AND WHY YOU ARE GOING THERE*

Crazy dreams

Let me introduce you to a fantastic person – many will know him, but for those that don't, you should do – he is an inspiration. Jeremy Gilley is an independent documentary filmmaker and in 1998 he had a crazy idea that turned into an enormous goal,

a goal bigger than any I have ever dreamed of and my guess is that it would be the same for you.

He decided to create a day of peace – a day when every war on the planet would stop for one day.

That is a crazy, pie in the sky and surely unachievable goal. But... He is achieving it!!

In 2001 the United Nations passed a resolution marking the 21st of September a global day of peace.

In 2007 even the Taliban agreed to it!!

Since then, this agreement – by all parties in Afghanistan – to one day of peace each year has resulted in the immunization against polio of 4.5 million children so far. On Peace Day 2006, 60 tons worth of food was dropped into previously inaccessible areas of Southern Sudan and on Peace Day 2007, 600,000 insecticide treated mosquito nets were delivered to children in the Democratic Republic of the Congo. These are just a few examples of what is being achieved on this day every year.

It's astonishing – however, as amazing as his cause is and certainly one that surely any sane person would support,

it is the process that Jeremy and many others like him have used to achieve what seem to be ridiculous unachievable goals.

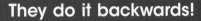

They do it backwards!

Jeremy didn't start with a goal to achieve peace in his local area and then when that worked step up to achieving peace in the UK, Europe and so on – no, he started at the end and then worked backwards.

Where would you start to achieve a goal this big? What would be the first thing you would have to do? Who would you have to involve? If he had started small he never would have considered getting the United Nations involved, might never thought about what humanitarian aid could be given on that day. In fact – the whole thing might never have happened.

You may have learnt in the past that you should make your goals realistic and achievable – Fantastic people just don't do that.

Post room workers who dream of being the boss one day, young sportspeople who dream of being the best in the world, small businesses that dream of dominating their market, independent documentary makers who decide to stop every war on the planet for one day!

Many people start getting nervous when I talk about this, feeling much more comfortable with nice, safe achievable goals. Why is this?

I think it's fear. The fear of failure is such a debilitating factor in life that so many of us would rather not do something, than try it and possibly fail.

The success/failure paradox

This is one of life's greatest paradoxes – the more you fear failure, the more likely you are to get it – because that fear will stop you doing the things that you need to do in order to be successful. However, the more you are prepared to fail – the more likely you are to be successful because you will take the chance and take action.

Think of it as a sports analogy –

Nobody can guarantee you will win the game, but I can 100% guarantee you can't win if you don't play!

IT'S OK TO NOT ACHIEVE YOUR GOALS!

It doesn't matter if you don't achieve your goals!

Has Jeremy Gilley achieved his goal – no – not yet. Will he ever? Will he ever achieve absolute peace and non-violence for one day – with every war, every abusive relationship, every bully out there, stopping what they do for 1 day – who knows, maybe – realistically we would have to say probably not – so, will he have failed?

Of course not – what he has done and will do in the future is fantastic, but the real question is whether anything at all would have been achieved if he hadn't been prepared to fail?

Goals are about momentum – they give you the focus to grow, to change, to learn new things. If you are not going on a journey, then there is no need to work out how to get there.

It doesn't actually matter if you don't get there. Of course you intend to, of course you want to, but we all know that life will throw up its own challenges – the 'spanner in the works', which will sometimes mean things don't work out how you intended. You will have still been moving though, meeting new people, learning new things – things that will help you in the next part of your life.

Look back at the 'failures' in your life and realise that they were not as bad as you thought – you learnt from them. So many people will tell you a horror story and then point out that they would not be where they are today if that so called failure hadn't happened.

The wonderful thing about this understanding is that it lifts the fear away from establishing goals. Particularly the big ones – the ones to fly! So what if you don't get there – you will have a lot of fun trying. It's better to have tried and failed, than never to have tried at all.

Where you put your focus is where you get your results remember – so if you want average, then set average goals, but if you want spectacular and amazing, then you had better start setting some spectacular and amazing goals.

Objective mapping

I am a big fan of Objective Mapping, developed from Tony Buzan's fantastic tool 'Mind Mapping'. It takes even the most ridiculous goals and breaks them down into small, easily achievable chunks.

You start by putting your focus in the centre – this could be anything – however big and unrealistic you want, but let's use something simple here that many people could relate to – weight loss.

Using positive language (much more important than you might think) it might read like this:

It's the 31st of May and I am now X (x = your target weight)

This complies with the rules of goals – It's specific, it has a deadline and it's positively stated as though it's already happened.

Now branch out with the primary action that has to be taken in order to achieve the central focus. Let's say, eat less, get fit and become healthier.

Next branch off from each primary action anything that has to be done to achieve it. So for example from 'get fit' you might have; join a gym, get a personal trainer, ride a bike to work, buy a bike, etc.

Prioritise and plan the action and away you go.

As you start taking action on more of those things, you will be getting closer and closer to the centre of the map, closer to achieving your focus.

Try it – try it with something simple and then try it with a crazy goal – the great thing about this technique is that even with a completely unrealistic goal in the centre there will always be something small on the outer edge of the map that you could do straight away – and you have started!

START AT THE END – FANTASTIC PEOPLE DO IT BACKWARDS!

45

WHERE YOU PUT YOUR FOCUS IS WHERE YOU GET YOUR RESULTS!

Passion is about focus - it's when we lose focus that we lose passion. Understand the difference between 'what' you do every day and 'why' you do it - if a street cleaner is focused on picking up rubbish then they will feel rubbish! If they focus on the positive effect they are having on their community they will feel fantastic!

BE EXCITED ABOUT WHERE YOU ARE GOING

It's not just about goals and where you are going - you have to be excited about 'why' you are going there to have the passion you need to be fantastic at whatever it is you are doing - I get excited about young people learning critical tools and skills that they can use throughout all areas of their life - that's why I happily do some of the things that I don't always enjoy doing - because I love 'why' I'm doing it!

FANTASTIC PEOPLE DO IT BACKWARDS!

Reach for the stars - you may never touch them but you will get off the ground trying. Fantastic people start with what might seem to be an unobtainable dream and then work backwards until they find something they can take action on that begins the journey - whether you achieve the dream or not you will still have taken action that will be giving you a degree of success.

Choose 3 goals from this chapter that you can take immediate action on:

1

2

3

4

FANTASTIC PEOPLE ARE CREATIVE

Change whether you like it or not

Here is a fact no one can dispute – we live in a rapidly changing world that shows no sign of slowing down – in fact, all the indicators point to an ever-increasing speed of change.

It's happening whether you like it or not. I do understand and share some of the concerns many people have about this. However, there is nothing we can do to stop it. Therefore we had better start to work out how to operate in this environment.

We have to be creative, and if you think you are not a creative person, then you had better start learning – quickly – because it's the only future I can see. Individuals and companies have to have the ability to react, to change fast, to have innovative and creative solutions as well as be creatively leading the field.

This isn't just about the work place – relationships are changing, parenting is changing – everything about the way we live our lives is changing – we all have to learn to love change as much as we might have hated it in the past.

I call this the creative revolution.

FOCUS

Focus on solutions not problems. If you only see barriers then you won't achieve anything. Is the problem that there isn't enough money to do what you want, or that you haven't yet come up with a more cost effective solution?

It's more ideas you need, not more money.

LISTEN

Listen – listen to your customers, your team, your friends, your kids – listen to everybody and everything. You need information – you need it to learn but you also need it to inspire your creativity. Your brain works with connections. One thought triggers another and so on. The more information you devour the more creative you will be as you spark off different things.

BE 'BUY' FOCUSED

If you are in business, you must listen to your customers – become 'buy' focused not sales focused. Think a bit more about what people want to buy, rather than just what we want to sell them!

NAÏVE LISTENING

Be open-minded, practice Naive Listening – I love that term. Listen naively – without knowledge or experience, because both those things, as valuable as they can be, will tend to give you a closed mind to new ideas.

CREATE

Now start being creative. The next few pages will give you some simple ideas on how to develop your creativity.

ENGAGE

Engage people – you need others – this new world is not one that you can survive in on your own – collaboration not competition is the key – find people to help you, people who understand and share your passion.

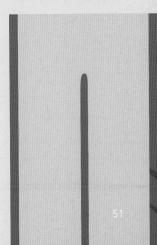

WE ALL HAVE TO LEARN TO LOVE CHANGE

ACT

Take action – all the creativity in the world is worth nothing if you don't have the courage to take action – remember the success/failure paradox – the more you fear failure the more likely you are to fail because you won't take action.

FUN

Finally, have fun doing it – for the same reason fun is the last of the 7 characteristics – if it's not fun you won't keep doing what you need to do. Make sure you are having fun!

Think outside the box

How many times have we heard that statement? But it sums up the creative process so well. When we are trying to come up with new ideas, we can get stuck in a mind set – a way of thinking which we can't break out of. We are actually excluding information because we have limited what we know to 'the box'.

It's like trying to get a spreadsheet to do a calculation without some of the relevant formulas. It will just go round and round coming up with the same answer, which is not the answer you want.

Add in a different formula and hey presto! – it will give you a different answer. This is what thinking outside of the box is – adding more information, which allows you to think differently about the situation.

I remember a great exercise from Tony Buzan – a genius who understands more about how to use the brain than anyone I have ever met. He gave us a minute to think of as many different ways as we could, to use a paper clip. Most of us came up with between 5 and 10. He then asked us if it had occurred to us that the paper clip could be any size and that we could do more than just change the shape by bending it – we could melt it down. At this point it became obvious that there were endless possibilities. The only thing that changed was the extra information we were given – which changed our box!

Creative thinking is simply learning how to add extra information to change the box that you are thinking within. This is why the listening part of the creative revolution is so important.

Creative thinking

Use creative techniques, like brainstorming. This is where you just throw any ideas and thoughts randomly onto a piece of paper, not stopping to think about whether they will work or if you have the budget etc. That all comes later – after the creative process you analyse each idea to see whether it can work, but not during the creative process.

Analysis during the creative process will kill creativity

The best way to really stretch yourself with brainstorming is to give yourself crazy time limits – see if you can come up with 30 solutions in one minute. The only way you can do this is to free yourself from the shackles that bind our minds. It is always easier to do this with other people, as you will spark off each other – so use your team, friends and family to help you be creative.

Bounce!

Find techniques that bounce you out of a fixed mind-set. I often use a technique called 'random word'. Just take a random word from a book and brainstorm solutions to your problem from that word. Remember it doesn't matter if everything is silly, it will automatically start you thinking outside of that fixed mind-set.

Creative note taking

Keep a small note pad with you at all times. You never know when your brain might decide to throw a solution at you. Or maybe you will see something that is just what you need. Keep that pad beside your bed too – it's amazing how creative our brains can be when we are half asleep.

Get into the habit of jotting your thoughts down in your pad – it will help to condition you towards a more creative way of thinking. It doesn't matter if the idea doesn't work – you are only writing it down. But as you do this more, you will notice you have more freedom in the way that you think.

GET INTO THE HABIT OF JOTTING YOUR THOUGHTS DOWN IN YOUR PAD – IT WILL HELP TO CONDITION YOU TOWARDS A MORE CREATIVE WAY OF THINKING

Let your ideas fail!

So many people tell me they are not creative – I can't accept this – I think what this really means is: "I'm not brave enough to give my ideas oxygen – to let them breathe, to let them live."

We all have ideas – however if those ideas never make it out of your mind and into the real world then they will fade and die. Creativity isn't just about having loads of ideas – it's about being prepared to let them fail.

Failure is a creative process:

The biggest barrier to creativity is fear – a fear of failure. Think of how many times you have talked yourself out of a good idea. Why is that? I guarantee it is because the voices in your head were telling you that it might be a stupid idea that might not work, that everyone would laugh.

Because of those voices, we never give those ideas oxygen. We don't let them out into the world to breathe, to live – to find out whether they would work.

Looking at failure differently will start to unlock your creativity.

Thomas Edison was once asked how he coped with the inevitable failure that scientist and inventor must face. "It's easy," he said.

"What you see as failure, I see as being successful at finding out it didn't work that way!"

Isn't that great? What a great way to look at failure. Try it. It really does make a huge difference.

YOUR MILLION DOLLAR IDEAS

Now apply the paradox to creativity. I have no way of proving this, but I think most people will have had their million dollar idea at least once in their life – actually I think we have probably had loads – however if you aren't prepared to nurture it, to feed it, give that idea a try or involve other people to help you and take the risk that it might not work, then you will never bring it to life.

But someone else might!!

Set failure goals!

I came across an outrageous idea once that is so crazy it works. Try it – it's very simple, set yourself failure goals! I know how that sounds but remember failure is NOT negative, it is just part of the creative process.

We are not talking about sloppy failure – failure because you didn't prepare properly or didn't do your research – no. This is stuff you tried that just didn't work – where you just didn't get the success you expected or hoped for.

Just remember how many times Colonel Sanders 'failed' trying to get a franchise deal for Kentucky Fried Chicken, (over 1000 if you didn't know). Walt Disney had many ideas that didn't work, even going bankrupt at one stage, but was still prepared to give the idea of an animated mouse a try! What about the post-it® note – it was developed from a failure at 3M® – they had created a glue that didn't stick!!

So just for fun, set yourself some failure goals. Try and get say, 5 a day.

To get 5 failures a day, you have to get your ideas out in the open. Go to a meeting and try to get people to laugh at 5 of your ideas. The only way you can achieve that is to put forward at least 5 ideas.

What if you wanted to go out on the town to meet new people, you could set yourself a goal of getting turned down twenty times. You would have to ask at least 20 people to achieve that goal. Surely if you asked twenty people for a dance, someone would say yes!

For me, this is the core foundation of creativity – overcome that fear of failure and you are ready to begin the creative process by giving your ideas oxygen – get them out of your head and be prepared for them to fail.

"The 1% that we call success comes from the 99% that we call failure"

Soichiro Honda

IT'S MORE IDEAS YOU NEED, NOT MORE MONEY

Are you focused on problems or solutions? Listen to the world with your eyes and your ears, listen with an open mind and you will get the inspiration you need for a solution. Now you can focus on creative solutions, engage other people to help you take action and have some fun doing it!

USE YOUR HEAD

Learn about how your brain works. We have this amazing creative resource we call a mind – it's astonishing what this 'mind' has created over the years. It's not about intelligence – it's simply about using your brain more, learning how to think creatively and then practicing it – anyone can do it – really – anyone!

GIVE YOUR IDEAS OXYGEN

Everybody is creative – it is impossible to get through the day without having creative ideas. However those ideas are no good if you don't give them oxygen – if you don't let them breathe. Get them out of your head, be brave enough to fail! It's the only way you can be successful. Creativity isn't just about coming up with ideas, it's having the courage to try things, even if the only success you get is to find out that, that one, didn't work!

Choose 3 goals from this chapter that you can take immediate action on:

1

2

3

5

FANTASTIC PEOPLE DELIGHT

The customers are revolting

Another revolution! This time it is about all of us as customers.

We are revolting!!

Whether you deal directly with customers in your job or not – the customer revolution affects all of us. You may not think you have anything to do with customers. But surely everybody does. My father-in-law drives a lorry for a supermarket chain – he has no real contact with customers, but he gets very upset if he sees a competitor's product in my fridge.

You see, he understands a basic principle – if too many people start buying his competitors' products he might be out of a job. It's as simple as that. Therefore, even though he wouldn't be seen as customer facing, he is as passionate about the customer as everyone should be.

Let's face it – it's quite a simple principle – if people don't 'buy' your company's product or service you don't have a job. That's as true in the national health service as it is for a retail store, or whether you work on your own in an office doing accounts or dealing directly with the customer.

But of course the way this affects every single one of us is quite simple – we are all customers.

The price experience match

Nowhere is the customer revolution more critical than with this principle.

If the experience you get when purchasing something does not match up to the price you are paying for it then you will not go back, which is of course the acid test for any business – returning customers.

It's quite simple, if I am going to pay £7 to £8 for a coffee and a sandwich – I want more than a coffee and a sandwich because I can get 'just' a coffee and a sandwich for £2 to £3.

So why on earth would I pay three times as much? For the experience – for the leather sofa, trained barista, pleasant service, free Wi-Fi, nice décor etc. So what happens if the sofa is dirty, my coffee isn't warm enough, nobody smiles or acknowledges me, the Wi-Fi isn't working and the décor is tired?

All I have is a very expensive (luke warm) coffee and sandwich!!

If the experience matches the price it can be astonishing what people are prepared to pay, but be under no illusion that if it doesn't, they just won't come back.

I have tried to use an environment we can all relate to here, but this could be in the form of an online purchase, a painter and decorator, the accounts department of a supplier or a utility provider as much as it could be using a hair salon, an airline, hotel, restaurant, retail store etc.

Don't serve people – delight them

When you have an attitude of delighting people, WOW-ing them, surprising, exciting and inspiring people rather than just serving them, you will also enjoy what you do more as well as be more successful. Where do you get that attitude?

Your passion – the reason why you are doing what you are doing!

FLOW is a great personal checklist to make sure you are always delighting people.

Make sure you always check on whether you are creating a fantastic **First** impression, that you always leave people with a fantastic **Last** impression, that you minimize and deal positively with any **Ouch's** the customer may receive and finally that you are always looking to see how you can **Wow** the customer every time.

CHECK YOUR FLOW DELIGHT HAS TO BE CONSISTENT YOU CAN'T JUST DELIGHT PEOPLE ON TUESDAYS!

The archer doesn't blame the target when they miss

This is my favourite quote about communication. I love it. It sums up exactly what great communication is all about. If you don't understand what I am communicating to you, it is no good me blaming you, I have to look at my aim. It's my aim that is wrong – not the target!

"How many times have I got to tell you?"

A question we have all heard as kids and it is very rarely answered. The answer is:

"You have to tell me as many times as it takes for me to understand."

Good communicators understand everyone is different. They take responsibility for getting across what they want to say, in a way that people will take on board. If your message isn't getting through, stop, listen, understand why and try a different approach.

THE HOUSE OF UNDERSTANDING

Understanding is the first step towards fantastic communication.

I have borrowed a tool from Transactional Analysis here and turned it into something I call the House of Understanding.

Think of this model as a dolls' house with the front open, showing four rooms inside. Each room represents an attitude of mind that we may have whilst communicating with another party.

Room 1 is called I'm ok, you're ok.

In this room 'my' attitude is: I am happy with who I am, I am aware of my strengths and confident that I am basically a good person. I do have weaknesses and some of them I am improving, however I understand that I am a normal human being and I can't be good at everything.

I don't make judgements without relevant information and recognise your right to a point of view – even if I disagree with it! I understand that you may be different from me. You might have different opinions to me, enjoy different things and want different things but it is not a case of right and wrong – just different.

I have a good life, even though there have been many not so good moments. I have made mistakes, done things I shouldn't have done, things I wish I hadn't. I've said things I wish I hadn't said (maybe to you) but I have learnt from those mistakes, put them behind me and moved on positively.

What about my attitude towards you – well it's very similar. I am happy with who you are, I am aware of your strengths and recognise that you are probably a good person, even if I may not be seeing that from you at a certain time. You have weaknesses but that's ok – so do I! You have a good life, although you have had your not so good moments. You have made mistakes, done things you shouldn't have done, things you wish you hadn't. You've said things you wish you hadn't said, maybe to me, but so have I. If it's ok for me to learn and move on, surely I have to let you do it too.

Recognise that other people have strengths, have a right to their opinions – even if you disagree with them. They also have weaknesses – but doesn't everybody? In fact, don't you?

Basically in this room your attitude is simply I'm ok and so are you.

There are essentially two elements to good communication – being confident enough to express your views, opinions or ideas and also being open-minded enough to listen to the other party's views.

It is quite obvious that you would be able to do both these things well in this room.

How about room 2?
I'm ok, you're not ok.

My attitude towards myself is the same as in room 1 apart from the judgements I make about you. You see, in this room I see you very differently. All I see are your weaknesses and although it's ok for me to have mine, I'm afraid I am going to judge you on yours! You have also made mistakes, done things you shouldn't have, said things you wish you hadn't, maybe to me – and I'm not going to forget it. I'm not going to move on with yours – I am never going to forgive you.

At its worst this room has all the 'ism's in it. Racism, sexism, ageism etc. I am not suggesting that anyone reading this book is at that level but I will say that in different ways we all spend some time in this room. If you drive a car, you know what I mean. You might make a genuine mistake as a driver yourself – after all, you are only a human being. But if someone else makes the same mistake, they are an idiot who shouldn't be allowed on the road!

We can all be guilty of making judgements without the facts – not listening to someone else's point of view because "they are wrong," or because "they don't know what they are talking about."

So how is the communication going to be in room 2? Will you have the confidence to say what you want to say? Definitely. But will you also listen to what others have to say? Probably not – it's not really worth it because you are the one who's right anyway!

Room 2 can be an aggressive room, with people expressing their opinions as facts – not listening to others and making judgements about people without the relevant information. Not great communication!

Room 3 is not a great room. I'm not ok, you're not ok.

This is the depressed state of mind. I guess we all pop in here every now and then in our lives but it's not a room you want to spend any length of time in. Quite obviously the communication is not good in here.

Finally, room 4, I'm not ok, you're ok.

It is in this room that we can feel intimidated, nervous or lacking in confidence, worried about what others will think of us, doubting ourselves. Unlike the other party, who seems full of confidence, knowledge, experience etc.

Their confidence can only make us feel more insecure as we begin to feel out of our depth. You may not want to admit it but everybody I have ever met agrees that they spend part of their life in this room – not feeling as good about themselves, compared to other people.

Will you listen to others in this room? Yes, you will because the other party seems so knowledgeable. But will you say what you think? Probably not – have you ever been in a meeting or training session, had an idea or thought pop in to your mind but not had enough confidence to voice it? You were in room 4!

There is only one room where good communication takes place.

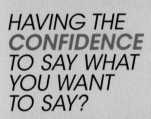

HAVING THE CONFIDENCE TO SAY WHAT YOU WANT TO SAY?

Room 1 – I'm ok, you're ok – it's the only room where you will both voice your opinion whilst also listening to the other's point of view.

The next time you find yourself in room 2 – making judgements or not listening, just press the pause button – stop for a moment and realise that you will never get anywhere in that room. Then mentally step across into room 1 and change your attitude.

If you find yourself in room 4, jump up, grab hold of the floor above you and haul yourself up into room 1 where you have every right to be – as much right as anyone.

An interesting thing about this model is that some people in room 4 who start to feel they are not being heard, feel that they have to go into room 2.

You don't – you just need to be more assertive (room 1) not aggressive (room 2).

In fact, I think that one of the reasons why so many people are un-assertive is that they think the only alternative is to act like people do in room 2. When you don't want to act aggressively, it seems easier to stay quietly in room 4 and let other people get their own way.

All you have to do is communicate assertively – not agressively.

FOR PEOPLE TO BE INTERESTED IN YOU, YOU HAVE TO BE INTERESTED IN THEM FIRST

People not things

We all love things – my wife loves it when I buy her flowers, I like the chocolate on my pillow in the hotel and the fancy coffee at my dentist.

However real delight – sustainable delight, comes from people not things.

If a new hotel reduced the interior design budget by 5% and spent that money on better training for the team, it would mean that the reception and bar are 5% less fancy than they might have been. However, the people who work there would be 100% better and I might stay in more hotels that delight me!

Make people feel good

Everyone likes positive feedback. Some people may pretend that they don't – but they do really. They may have a belief somewhere that says it's cool to be negative, to not show any emotion, to think that anything positive is shallow and can't be trusted. However, underneath all that, they still respond to positive communication, even if they pretend they don't.

It's a simple rule – if someone feels good about themselves and their relationship with you, they are more likely to help you.

It's called rapport.

Have you ever tried to get the miserable waiter/receptionist etc., to smile – it's amazing when you succeed – they can literally transform in front of your very eyes!

LEARN TO LISTEN

Engage people

This is not just some 'be nice to people' campaign here, although as a Londoner, I do sometimes love saying good morning to people on the tube, just to see their reaction! It's just a fact that if you make people smile they will be more helpful to you in general (not always on the London Underground though!).

Coming home from work to a smile rather than a list of things you haven't done; being genuinely interested in a teenagers' life rather than seeing them as some sort of alien; being greeted warmly at a meeting; making a customer feel fantastic about themselves; commenting positively on a colleagues' work – all those things and more must surely make a difference!

I feel that communication is one of – if not the most – important skills in life.

Listening is the most important communication skill

Which makes listening pretty important in the whole scheme of things!!

If you want to engage people, you have to start by listening to them.

What are their interests, their views, what are their goals and their dreams?

When you genuinely listen to people, you are already on the way to making them smile – everybody wants to be listened to – to feel as though their thoughts or opinions matter.

There are two types of listening we should practice. Firstly, using our ears. Think about the following rules of good listening and ask yourself how you do.

Listen with your ears

1. Give complete attention and focus to the person speaking

2. Give good eye contact and use appropriate body language

3. Make listening noises to encourage, "Mm, aha, really"

4. Think only about what they are saying, not about what you are going to say when they have finished

5. Never interrupt

6. Never finish people's sentences

7. Think briefly about what they have said and your opinions on it before responding

So, how did you do? Is it time to start learning to listen?

The listening switch

This a great tool to help remind you to really listen to people.

Imagine you have a switch on the side of your head – a listening switch. When somebody starts talking to you and you need information from them, use the switch as a trigger to remind you to consciously listen to them. Flip the switch, focus on them, concentrate on what they are saying, and really LISTEN!

If you get into the habit of doing this, it will start to happen naturally. But start now. You have people talking to you every day – it's a great opportunity for you to develop one of the most important skills in life.

Listen with your eyes

The second way you need to learn to listen is with your eyes.

This is fascinating. When you learn to use your eyes to listen to people, it is amazing how much information you can get. There are two areas I want you to think about here.

Firstly, you have to understand which part of their brain someone is using to process information, which then allows you to communicate much more effectively with them.

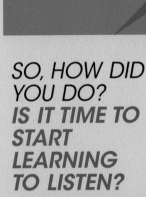

SO, HOW DID YOU DO? IS IT TIME TO START LEARNING TO LISTEN?

71

There are three ways we process information inside our heads.

We visualise it, hear it, or we feel it. If someone is using the visual part of their brain to listen to you, they will not understand you – they will not SEE what you mean – if you do not use visual references when explaining something.

You need to know how they are thinking. Watch people's eyes and they give you all the clues you need. When someone is visualising they either gaze off into the distance, or more usually, they glance upwards.

If someone is listening inside his or her head, they will glance to the side, and when they are experiencing a feeling, they will look down. If you bother to take notice of this, and adjust your communication accordingly, you will be amazed by the results.

Secondly, become more aware of your own, and other people's body language. It's not a perfect science, but it does give you many pointers that are very helpful to great communication.

Learn to recognise when someone is feeling nervous, unhappy, in a hurry, stressed etc., and you will be in a much better position to help them smile. For example, the sales person who doesn't realise their customer is pushed for time will just annoy them, as against the person who recognises it and then makes an effort to be as quick as they can.

I would strongly recommend Alan Pease's great book 'Body Language'. It's a lot of fun and will give you some real insights into what people are telling you.

SAY IT WITH FLOWERS!

The language we use has a powerful impact on both the people we are communicating with and of course ourselves. We do listen to ourselves!

The effect that language has on the way we operate is amazing. When you understand it, you become very careful about what you say to yourself and to others.

The unconscious part of the brain that processes the information you receive, from yourself or others, does not have the capability to make decisions. It simply looks in its' memory banks for the definition it has for those words and acts accordingly.

Put your right arm up in the air now. OK, put it down now.

Now, assuming you just did that – this is what happened. Information gets to your brain via one or more of your senses. In this case, you read it, so it was through sight, but if I had said it, then it would have been through your ears.

That information was then processed and you acted upon it. Some of that took place at a conscious level – maybe you had to take a moment to think about right or left – but most of it happened at an un-conscious or sub-conscious level. Your brain worked the muscles needed to complete that task, but you were not aware of it – it was not at a conscious level.

This is obviously happening all the time. What it tells us, is that there is some sort of 'brain dictionary' that understands "right arm up" and what it means.

Do you understand Japanese, or Russian? What if I asked you to do the same thing in a language you didn't understand? What would happen – nothing – because your brain wouldn't understand the words and therefore not be able to process them.

DON'T RELY ON 'THINGS' TO DELIGHT PEOPLE
YOU DO IT – WITH GREAT COMMUNICATION!

When your brain understands the words that are fed into it, it reacts accordingly.

This is so important as it explains why listening to positive communication starts to make you feel more positive but... the same is true for negative communication – you feel more negative. If you say to yourself "I'm feeling really knackered", your brain understands what "knackered" means – it knows what it feels like and so will then act in that way, making you feel even more knackered.

Start to listen to people and you will notice how negative we can be in what we say to ourselves, and to other people. Unfortunately, you will see this a lot with children. If you tell a child they are "bad" for long enough, what will you get?

A bad child!

Improve the words you use. It's not just about being over the top positive all the time – it's just about understanding how the 'brain dictionary' will interpret the words you use.

Firstly, start to make your language more helpful. Use positive alternatives such as "I need to stay awake," rather than "I mustn't fall asleep." "Make sure I remember..." not "Make sure I don't forget."

It's interesting to notice what happens when you use words like "don't" or "mustn't". Say to yourself: "Don't think of an elephant". What happens? You think of an elephant! In fact you can't "not think of an elephant," without thinking of one!

So when you say, "don't forget", your brain thinks about forgetting, and what is the brain dictionary's definition of forget?

Notice how some people respond to a simple "How are you?" "Not bad" is a favourite answer – all your brain understands is "bad"! How many times a day does that happen – every day? What a great message you are giving yourself, let alone the people who are asking.

WRITE A LIST OF THE NEGATIVE WORDS OR PHRASES THAT YOU USE AND FIND POSITIVE ALTERNATIVES FOR THEM.

YOU WILL NOTICE A DRAMATIC DIFFERENCE IN THE EFFECT YOUR COMMUNICATION HAS ON BOTH YOURSELF AND OTHERS.

DON'T SERVE PEOPLE – DELIGHT THEM

Service is dead – long live delight! As customers, we are all revolting – revolting against paying decent money for things and not getting the experience we deserve whilst spending our hard earned money. If you have anything to do with customers, then you best be delighting them otherwise they just won't come back and eventually, you'll be out of a job/out of business – it's as simple as that!

THE ARCHER DOESN'T BLAME THE TARGET WHEN THEY MISS

Communication is one of the most important skills in life and certainly when you need to engage people, whether they are customers, colleagues, friends or family – fantastic communication is the key. The secret to great communication is understanding. Step into other people's shoes and understand them. Be aware of how they are thinking or feeling. If your message isn't hitting the target it is your aim that is wrong!

MAKE PEOPLE FEEL GOOD

Is life really this simple – actually I truly think it is. When you make people feel good they are more likely to help you and we all need help. The key here is attention – if you want people to pay attention to you then you have to pay attention to them, and that starts with listening, really listening to people. Then use positive language. Have the confidence to sincerely compliment people and make people feel good.

Choose 3 goals from this chapter that you can take immediate action on:

1

2

3

6

FANTASTIC PEOPLE ARE PERFORMERS

6

FANTASTIC
PEOPLE ARE
PERFORMERS

Fantastic people are performers

All along I have said that learning without action is pointless – but why does this happen so much – why do we not take the action that we know will make a difference – it's a lack of confidence.

So many people say to me that they agree with everything I teach, but they don't feel confident enough to put it into action.

THE SECRET OF CONFIDENT PEOPLE: THEY ACT – THEY PRETEND!

The actress Julia Roberts once told a group of drama students that she could get terribly nervous at auditions.

When a student asked how she deals with those nerves, she replied, "I'm an actress – I act. I act confident, and the more you act confident, the more confident you become."

As I have already mentioned, there are times when you may be feeling tired or hung-over at work, but you know that you can't be like that so you pretend you are OK. You act. Isn't it amazing how you can change the way you feel?

Or maybe you have done it the other way? When you were younger – you didn't want to go to school one day, so you pretended that you didn't feel well. You acted ill. In fact, you may have turned in such an Oscar winning performance that you actually started to feel ill!

An actor isn't sad, they are just acting sad. They don't love that person, they are simply acting – pretending.

However – they do it so well we believe it. They are able to get into the right state of mind to make us believe it.

That is what happens when you act yourself.

If you act confidently, then you start to feel confident which in turn makes others feel that you are confident.

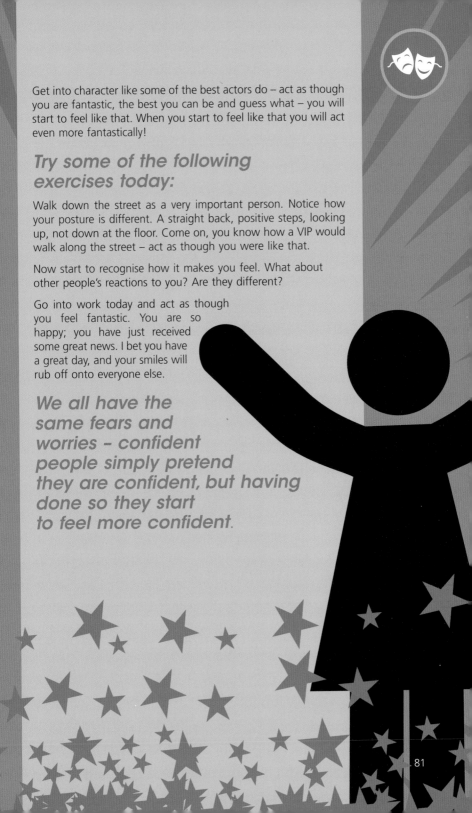

Get into character like some of the best actors do – act as though you are fantastic, the best you can be and guess what – you will start to feel like that. When you start to feel like that you will act even more fantastically!

Try some of the following exercises today:

Walk down the street as a very important person. Notice how your posture is different. A straight back, positive steps, looking up, not down at the floor. Come on, you know how a VIP would walk along the street – act as though you were like that.

Now start to recognise how it makes you feel. What about other people's reactions to you? Are they different?

Go into work today and act as though you feel fantastic. You are so happy; you have just received some great news. I bet you have a great day, and your smiles will rub off onto everyone else.

We all have the same fears and worries – confident people simply pretend they are confident, but having done so they start to feel more confident.

Do it right consistently

I have always believed that we can all do it right! We can all be fantastic at whatever it is we want to do – the difference between the successful people and everyone else is that they do it right – they are fantastic – CONSISTENTLY.

But how?

Are they sub-human – somehow different from the rest of us? Maybe they don't get sick, feel tired, have hangovers, relationship problems or bad moods?

Or,

are they exactly the same as everyone else, having the same stuff happening in their lives as everyone else, but just dealing with it differently?

Successful people take 'fantastic' action consistently by performing. They understand that the world is a stage and they need to be performers on it.

We all have off days, but when you understand the importance of consistency, you quickly learn to perform – to act. This is not living a lie, it's simply making a decision to get on with it.

We all have a choice – I can decide to spend the day with a hangover, or decide not to have it. I'm human like anybody and sometimes I decide to have it! But, only if it doesn't affect me being fantastic at work or as a dad, husband or friend.

That's when I have to 'act' – but the amazing thing is that when I make the decision to act better – I start to feel better!

Do people trust you?

You need people to trust you – your customers, colleagues, friends and family. Why? Because whatever you may think, you can't do it on your own – we all need people, but to get help, support and respect from people, they need to trust you.

How do we earn that trust?

By acting consistently! Turn it around and you will clearly see that the people you don't trust in your life are not consistent. I don't mean a nasty horrible distrust, just simply for instance – the person at work who you can't guarantee will get a job done on time, or the friend who may or may not turn up when they say they will.

They can do it right, they just don't do it right – consistently.

Passion

The discipline needed to be consistent, to persevere when things get tough, comes from your passion.

We have obviously discussed this in detail in chapter 3 but if consistency and self-discipline are issues for you then please go back and re-read that chapter.

Remember, the key is the 'why'. If your 'why' is powerful enough it is easy to have the discipline needed to be consistent.

I always use vegetarians as an example of amazing consistency and self-discipline. They usually look at me strangely when I suggest this, as of course to them they are not consciously being self-disciplined – they just don't eat meat.

But they will have a powerful reason 'why'. Faith, moral issues, health – whatever the reason, it's powerful enough for them to make a choice every day with amazing consistency. I don't know many vegetarians who have the odd sneaky fillet steak or lamb chop. But it comes easy to them because of the reason why they are doing it.

IF YOU FIND A REASON TO BE FANTASTIC THAT IS POWERFUL ENOUGH, CONSISTENCY AND SELF-DISCIPLINE WILL NEVER BE AN ISSUE

DOGASHI

Let me introduce you to DOGASHI.

What is it?

DOGASHI is a wonderful ancient eastern technique that has the most amazing impact on your ability to take action in your life.

We all know taking action is not always as easy as it seems.

We all intend to do the things that we decide to do, but so often it doesn't happen. Not just the big things in life either. Think about the times you were going to send someone a thank you card – but didn't, or what about those phone calls that you need to make, but keep putting off?

It's the voices!!

I remember a visit to my dentist once, many years ago before I knew about DOGASHI. I was late for my appointment and I knew that I had messed up her day. She was really nice about it, but I still felt guilty and as I lay there in the chair, I remembered that there was a flower stall outside the front door. As an apology for being late and a thank you for being so nice about it, I decided to get her some flowers. A nice thing to do, I'm sure you agree.

Then the voices started!

You know – the voices in our head that start to talk us out of things, which introduce doubts and fear. "She'll think you fancy her if you get her flowers", "She'll be embarrassed", "You'll be embarrassed next time you see her", "What will the receptionist think?" Recognise any of those? Well, that's what started in my head when I decided to get her some flowers.

The sad thing is, I let them win – I didn't get the flowers!

If you want to take action – even with the little things in life – then you have to deal with those voices, and shut them up.

You see, most of the time the voices are wrong!! I don't think she'd have thought I fancied her, or been embarrassed, I think she would have been over the moon! It would have been a nice thing to happen on a stressful busy day.

So, how does DOGASHI work?

It silences the voices, enables you to step past them and do what you want to do. It helps you to learn something, from this book perhaps, and put it into action – without worrying what other people say or think about your new behaviour. It could help you to overcome the peer pressure that is making you; drink too much, party too hard, or take drugs that don't help you. You know what I mean. We have all been in a situation where we have wanted to go home early from a night out or someone wanted us to do something we didn't want to – but the voices are telling us that our friends will think us boring, etc.

DOGASHI is simply a way to remind yourself that they are only voices in your head. Sure, sometimes they might be right and you should listen to them, but in my experience DOGASHI always helps me recognise the ones that are just knocking me back, the ones that are stopping me taking the action I should do.

I FIBBED!!

Sorry – I fibbed a bit about DOGASHI. It isn't really an ancient eastern technique. I just thought that it added some intrigue. It does sound like it though doesn't it – "DOGASHI" – but I actually made it up! I wanted a word that I could use to shut the voices up, and DOGASHI is actually a statement that I was using, shortened down to make it easier, and perhaps nicer to use.

You see DOGASHI is short for – DOn't Give A SHI*! That's what you have to say to those voices sometimes when they are trying to stop you taking action – DOGASHI – I don't give a s**t – I'm still going to do it!

I am sure you understand the manner in which I mean this statement. DOGASHI is not about other people. It's not about being arrogant or aggressive. You are not saying that you don't care about other people, or their feelings.

There you go – DOGASHI – try it, it's fantastic. Shut those voices up and have the confidence to take action.

DOGASHI IS SIMPLY ABOUT GETTING RID OF THE VOICES IN YOUR HEAD THAT ARE HOLDING YOU BACK. WHEN YOU USE IT, YOU INSTINCTIVELY KNOW THAT THOSE VOICES ARE WRONG

THE SECRET OF CONFIDENT PEOPLE – THEY PRETEND!

Zero action = Zero results. Why don't people take action? Fear! Worry! No confidence! We all have the same fears and worries, even so-called confident people. But as you begin to simply pretend you are confident, you start to feel more confident and then feel able to overcome your fears and take action.

DO IT RIGHT CONSISTENTLY

Consistency is key – however well you do something your success will come from doing it well and consistently – in your job or your life this rule is critical. You can't just be a great parent at weekends and it's no good just delighting customers on Tuesdays! However we are humans not machines, therefore we will not always feel able to be consistent. The answer is in the performer – you sometimes have to act, to pretend, but when you do – guess what – you actually start to 'act' differently!!

SHUT THE VOICES UP!

Are the fears that stop you taking action real?

Mostly, they aren't! We make them up in our heads, we watch movies of everything going wrong and listen to the voices in our heads that try and talk us out of things. Take control of your mind – sometimes you need to listen and sometimes the advice is good, but not always. Learn to distinguish the difference between experience/wisdom and fear.

When it is the fear talking, shut the voices up with Dogashi and take action.

Choose 3 goals from this chapter that you can take immediate action on:

1

2

3

7

FANTASTIC PEOPLE ARE ALIVE INSIDE

Alive inside

If you want to be alive on the outside, living your life to the full, being fantastic at what you do, then you have to be alive on the inside!

We all need to be motivated and enjoy praise and encouragement from others, but if you have taken anything at all from this book, surely it is the fact that 'if it's to be – it's up to me'.

We have to take responsibility for our life, and what happens in it.

The same is true for our motivation. If we want to be alive on the outside, living our life to the full, then we have to be alive on the inside!

STOP WAITING TO BE MOTIVATED!

Are you waiting to be motivated? That's what I call external motivation, motivation from an external source. External motivation is great and we all enjoy it when someone or something excites and inspires us. The problem is that you have no control over it – you never know when it's going to happen, so if you are not careful you can waste a lot of time waiting for it. Do you recognise any of these statements?

"I'm just not motivated at the moment"

"I need motivation"

"Nothing is motivating me"

The 'sit on the edge of the bed talk'

Internal motivation is when you take responsibility for your own motivation. I call it 'the sit on the edge of the bed talk'! It's simply when you sit, by yourself, on the edge of your bed, and give yourself a good talking to!

That's what being alive inside is – it's taking control of your motivation – the driving factor in whatever you want to achieve. You can't leave it to chance – it's too important for that.

Motivate your mind

But what do I do when I sit there? I hear some of you ask. You motivate your mind – you have to get your mind operating in a way that looks at things the right way. We have all heard the 'glass half full' analogy. How do you look at life? Is your glass half full or half empty? It really is as simple as that. Here are some ways to help you do that:

Focus on your strengths

We all have weaknesses, we all screw up, we all do or say things we wish we hadn't. However if all you ever do is look at those things you will find it difficult to motivate yourself. Do you remember the post- it® note exercise we did earlier in the book? Are you spending so much time focusing on what you don't do well that you don't have time to look at what your strengths are? Remind yourself of what you are good at, what you enjoy, what inspires and excites you rather than just the crappy stuff.

Solutions not problems

We all have problems, however if you sit there on the edge of the bed thinking about how many problems you have, it's no wonder you aren't motivated. Spend the time thinking about solutions, be creative, use your imagination – you can try anything in your imagination. You might not actually find a solution yet, but I guarantee you will feel more 'Alive Inside' if you are looking for one rather than just getting depressed by the problem.

How do I work?

To really take control of the way you feel and act, you have to understand how you work. I would not consider myself a computer expert – all I know is which buttons to press to make it do what I want.

However if a computer 'expert' sat with me for a couple of hours and watched me work, I am sure he could show me lots of short cuts and ways to make me more efficient. (What are those 'F' buttons for anyway?!)

Well it's the same with the way we use that most powerful and amazing 'computer' we have in our lives – the one we call a brain. What if we knew how to use it a bit more efficiently? What sort of difference might that make?

Well here we are – how we 'work' in 4 words:

Why do we act the way we do?

The way people act depends on their state of mind. If you have a confident state of mind, you will act confidently, whereas if you have a fearful state of mind it will affect your action negatively.

But where does that state of mind come from? It comes from our belief system. If you believe that crossing the road is a dangerous thing to do, you will have a fearful state of mind, which will result in very cautious action as you cross the road.

References

What are our beliefs based upon? They are based upon our references. I call them movies – where we have recorded everything that has ever happened to us, both good and bad. We play these over and over again in our mind, sometimes without realising we are doing it. These movies influence our beliefs, which in turn influences our state of mind and ultimately determines the way we act.

Made up movies

Many of these references are based on actual experiences that have happened to us – maybe you were hit by a car crossing the road which has given you the belief that crossing the road is dangerous...

However where it gets interesting is when you understand that many of the movies we watch that are literally shaping our lives, have not actually happened – we made them up!

Do you have a food that you have a negative belief about. You may never have eaten it, but have created a movie about what you think it would be like to eat. My one is snails! I have never eaten one but have created a movie that tells me they would be slimy and horrible. It doesn't matter whether it is right or wrong, it doesn't matter whether it is real or not, that movie will still create a belief, which influences your state of mind that determines your action.

Change your movies

So what happens if we watch different movies – you get a different belief and so on. The great thing is, we just agreed we have movies that affect us even if they are not real – so why not make some up – they will be just as powerful, as if they were real.

Understanding this will also help your communication with other people as we all operate the same way. Therefore if you want to change your own action or somebody else's, the procedure is the same.

You have to change the movie to change the belief – to change the state of mind, in order to change the action.

Here are the 4 words

our *REFERENCES*
create our *BELIEFS*
which influence our *STATE*
and determine how we *ACT*

Daydream with a purpose

If these movies are the drivers, what can we do to make them more dynamic, more motivating?

Firstly you have to make your movie – you have done this before – it's called daydreaming. Remember that thing they kept telling us not to do at school!

Although to be fair this is daydreaming with a purpose.

What belief do you need to change? Do you believe that a colleague is intimidating? What movie are you watching? I guarantee it is a movie of them being intimidating!

What if you made up a movie of them as a puppet wearing silly clothes and doing a daft dance on the palm of your hand? Are you smiling? If you are, I'm sure this is not the response you would normally have when thinking about that person! You created a different movie and it has created a different response.

More positively, what if we took something that you want to be more motivated to do. Create a movie of you doing it, enjoying it and being motivated by it.

Be a movie director

Now start to direct it. Make it more powerful. Remember we are talking about being alive inside here. Keep manipulating the movie until you really start to notice your motivation levels increase.

Be 'in' your movie

Are you watching yourself as though you are at the movies watching it on screen, or are you in the movie with everything happening around you? You will always be more motivated when you are what is called 'associated' – inside the movie, rather than just watching it.

Turn up the controls

What about the colours, brightness, size? What happens if you make it bigger, bolder, brighter? What can you change to make it more exciting in your mind? Are there phrases, words or soundtracks that would motivate you to achieve this goal – then add them in – remember it's all in your mind, it's your imagination so you can do anything!

Remember DOGASHI. Just do it. All you are doing is what any self respecting sports person or entertainer would do to push their motivation and energy up to the level they need, to perform at the highest standard.

Now whenever you need to increase your motivation to achieve your goal, think about the movie. Make the adjustments you need to amplify it, enjoy it, get excited by it, get 'alive inside' and then use that motivation to get on and do it!

For example: You can't be motivated to go to the gym when in your head you are watching a dull movie of yourself, trudging away on the treadmill. If this is then accompanied by an audio tape saying things like; "it's cold outside and nice and warm in this bed – there's always tomorrow" – it's not really any surprise that you're not getting to the gym.

So, let's make a new movie – a bright, large, vibrant movie of you working hard at the gym listening to great music. Then you're walking out, feeling that great buzz and satisfaction you get when you have been. And what if the audio is reminding you of how good you feel when you do go and why you are doing it in the first place? There are no guarantees of course, but surely you stand a better chance of success with this frame of mind.

Change your mind, literally, and you will start to get control of your attitudes and moods to help you be more motivated – to be alive inside.

REMEMBER DOGASHI. JUST DO IT

STOP WAITING TO BE MOTIVATED!

How can you be alive on the outside – if you aren't alive on the inside? Take responsibility for your own motivation. Everybody understands that nothing happens without motivation. If you are relying on external motivation, you have no control over when it will happen. Stop 'waiting' to be motivated and start taking responsibility for your own motivational levels if you want to be successful at what you do.

CHANGE YOUR MIND

Any action we take depends on our state of mind, which is determined by our beliefs. If you believe rain is horrible, then you will be de-motivated when it rains. However if you live where rain means a matter of life or death, you have a different belief and will therefore have a different state of mind when it rains – resulting in a different action. Our beliefs come from our references in our mind – the movies. Many of these movies are made up – they aren't real but they still affect us!

BE A MOVIE DIRECTOR

Change the movies! Watch different ones – maybe they are the good ones we forget to watch or perhaps you have to make some up. After all, we make up lots of scary horrible ones, so why not make up some positive ones that will put you into the right frame of mind to take action. Be a movie director – make up your own movies, but make them fantastic.

Choose 3 goals from this chapter that you can take immediate action on:

1

2

3

8

FANTASTIC PEOPLE ARE ALWAYS LEARNING

Are you in control of time or....

The biggest excuse people give me for not learning more is "I don't have the time".

I do understand, I am living in the same world as everyone else and there is no question there is more pressure on our time than ever before. All those time saving devices are just allowing us to fit more in!

Are you in control of time or is time in control of you? I think we all know how most people would answer that. Time will control us if we let it. Are you constantly saying things like: "I need more time." "There are not enough hours in the day, days in the week."

Do you feel out of control, just making deadlines by the skin of your teeth or maybe not making them at all? Are you getting the quality time you want in your life – with family, friends and in your relationships? Are there so many things that you want to do but you – just don't have the time?

However – there is an interesting fact about time – it is the great equaliser. In the short term, we all have the same – every being on the planet.

We all have the same amount of time – 24 hours a day, 7 days a week.

We have to stop saying there is not enough time, not enough hours in the day, days in the week etc. There is enough time – there are 24 hours a day and 7 days a week – the same for everybody.

What we have to address is that we sometimes aren't using the time available to us well! That's very different to not having enough time, because you can actually do something about it!!

Look at your day, look at your week. Where are you wasting time and where can you grab the time to use more productively in your life?

An hour less TV or internet surfing a day would give you the equivalent of an extra 45 working days per year! Get up 30 minutes earlier in the morning or spend 15 minutes a day doing something you think you don't have time for. Anyone can find 15 minutes a day, however busy they are.

Try the sums yourself with whatever you feel you might be wasting time with. The formula is simple – the hours spent per week, times 52, divided by 8 (for a working day) or 16 (for a waking day). Then to really frighten yourself – times it by 10, 20, or 30 years to see how much of your life you are spending doing that thing which you have already indicated is a waste of time.

Realistic planning

Make sure you plan your time realistically. So much time is lost through poor planning and preparation – not being realistic with how long a task will take. I still hear people say: "I'm just going to pop to the post office quickly." How often do you visit the post office quickly?! Are you one of those people that allow 30 minutes to do a half hour journey? Life just doesn't work like that.

Prioritise

Most people today think we have too much to do. Well, I could double your workload and do you know, it would make no difference to you. It would in your head but not in actuality. Sure it would freak you out and make you think; "If I can't manage what I have at the moment, how will I manage double?"

But in reality it works like this:

If you have ten tasks to do, how many can you do now? One – is the answer. So it doesn't matter if you have 20 tasks, or even 200, you can still only do one.

The key to your effectiveness is the decision you make as to which you choose to do first.

ANYONE CAN FIND 15 MINUTES A DAY, HOWEVER BUSY THEY ARE

I heard a statistic once, which astonished me at the time. Having become more aware of it though, I now realize it is probably about right. Around 60-70% of the time issues we have are down to the thief of time – procrastination – putting off till later, what we could or should be doing now.

This is different from prioritising, where you are making good decisions about doing one task before another.

The thief of time is when you are making bad decisions.

Do you have piles?

Well the piles I'm talking about are the ones on the corner of your desk and beside the microwave at home. The 'later' piles.

We all know how it works. You sit down in the morning, open your post, read something that needs action and say to yourself: "Mmm, that looks interesting, I'll deal with that later." Then it goes on the 'later' pile.

That's not prioritising, it's procrastination.

The thief of time shows itself in so many other areas – putting off the simple task of backing up your computer for instance. This as we all know, becomes a major time consuming job if not done regularly and then... Well we've all experienced what is guaranteed to happen – all that lost data – and what are the implications of that? Filing is a classic. And what about expenses?

Any of you that spend a lot of time in the car may recognise this one. The petrol gauge is flashing empty, the trip computer warning you that you need petrol.

"I'm sure I can make it past one more junction", we say to ourselves as we sail past the garage. It's almost as though we are trying to push it as far as we can, like some kind of dare.

Well we all know the end to that story.

It happens at home as well. Some people seem to think that if they don't open the bills but just put them on that pile, they don't have to pay them! Why does procrastination have such a critical effect on our time?

Simply because when you put something off till later, it always ends up taking longer than it would have done had you seen to it immediately.

How long does it take to rinse a coffee mug in the morning? A few seconds. But how long does it take to wash up that mug if you left it till later that day? A few moments – but that's just it. It's the few seconds versus the few moments. If we take that principle and run it through everything we are putting off till later, then it is easy to see where all the time is going.

So, what do we do? Well there is a simple phrase that I use which really helps me here and it consistently runs over in my mind. Three words that could literally change your life:

Do it now

Adopt this simple attitude and see the small stuff vanish off into the distance – the stuff that should never get near a list and does not need to be prioritised or planned – just actioned.

Finally, a question I'm often asked: "But what do you do if you can't do it right now?" Someone on a seminar answered this perfectly once – she said: "You decide which 'now' you are going to do it in." Now that's prioritising.

It's the word 'later' that is the problem. It's too vague, too unspecific. If you picked up a magazine and saw an article that interested you but you were about to go into a meeting, you wouldn't 'do it now'. The problem is, if you say: "That looks interesting, I'll read it later." You know as well as I do, you'll probably never read it.

Taking the advice of the delegate on my seminar – deciding which 'now' you are going to do it in, you should really say: "That looks interesting. I'll read it at lunchtime." Then at least you have a chance.

That's all it is though. I know it's crazy out there and you may not even get a lunch break today. None of this is guaranteed. All you are doing is shortening the odds. If you give yourself a better chance, surely it's worth it in order to get more control over time.

Set learning goals

The wonderful thing about the world of information today, can also be a problem if you don't manage it well enough.

The amazing wealth of information that is available to every single one of us via the internet, books, videos etc., means there is no excuse for ignorance anymore. However, there is so much stuff to learn in so many different areas that if you are not focused, if you don't have learning goals, you will waste loads of time.

Imagine just typing 'learn' into the Google or YouTube search box. I tried it and Google gave me 3,510,000,000 results!

Or walking into a bookshop and asking for a book to learn something!

What specifically do you need or want to learn?

What is going to help me be more fantastic at what I want to do?

Use the Fantastic Audit in chapter 10 to help you here. Set learning goals to make sure you are focused, otherwise the danger will be that you become so motivated to learn new stuff that you have no strategy – you are just learning randomly.

Focus on strengths

Remember to focus on what you are good at as well as what needs to improve. I sometimes feel that there is so much focus on what we don't do well that we miss the opportunity to develop both other people's and our own strengths.

I'm not saying we should ignore the things that need to improve, just that if we put a similar amount of focus on our strengths then we would really start to fly – the 100-metre sprinter wins the gold medal because they developed their strength of running fast, not by doing something they aren't very good at!

Set new year learning goals

I always start each year with a new learning focus – What do I want to learn about, this year? I normally have two focuses; one is to do with my work, my business. The other is to do with me as an individual, in my life generally. It means that I am constantly learning something new, which gives me the energy and motivation to always be striving to be fantastic.

How are you going to learn?

Now you know what you want to learn/develop you can start your research. Decide how you are going to learn what you need. Will it be from a book? If so, which? Or a course? Maybe you can get what you need from the internet through YouTube etc.

15 Minutes a day to change your life

This tool literally has the power to change your life.

I set myself a goal 30 years ago, to learn for a minimum of 15 minutes a day. To read something from a learning book or magazine, listen to or watch something that I can learn from. I stick to it religiously.

Fifteen minutes worth of learning a day is a minimum of 90 hours a year!!

That's a lot of learning! In fact it is the equivalent of a 1-day training course every month!! Project that forward 10 years and think about the impact a minimum of 900 hours focused learning would have on you and your life.

Anybody can find 15 minutes a day. Try it – use your preferred medium of learning. It will change the level of information you take on board dramatically.

THIS TOOL LITERALLY HAS THE POWER TO CHANGE YOUR LIFE

EVERYBODY ON THE PLANET HAS 24 HOURS A DAY, 7 DAYS A WEEK

Are you in control of time or is it controlling you? We all have the same amount of time available to us. Catch the 'Thief of Time' – have a 'Do it Now' attitude. Prioritise ruthlessly and be realistic with the way you plan your time to take back control.

SET LEARNING GOALS

There is so much information available to us today in so many different mediums that nobody has the excuse for not constantly learning. However, because of this it is essential that you are very focused. Set learning goals and spend the next 12 months completely focused on learning 2 or 3 completely new things to add to your life.

15 MINUTES A DAY TO CHANGE YOUR LIFE

Just 15 minutes a day learning, is the equivalent to over 90 hours of learning a year! If that was all you did, (you would probably do more of course) can you imagine the amount of knowledge and wisdom you could amass in a lifetime.

Now that would literally 'change your life'!

Choose 3 goals from this chapter that you can take immediate action on:

1

2

3

9

FANTASTIC PEOPLE ARE HAVING FUN!

What's fun for you?

The final characteristic is arguably the most important, as it's so difficult to keep the fantastic revolution going without it.

Let's face it, if you're not having fun, what's the point!

Anybody who is fantastic at what they do, must be having fun. It's a cycle – you have to be having fun in order to be fantastic, and if you are being fantastic – you are having fun. We normally talk about breaking out of a cycle, but not this one. What a great way to spend your life!

Have fun

It is always my sign off. I didn't realise it until someone pointed it out to me. You know how some people always say; "see ya" when they leave you, or "take care". It's just a habit and as this friend pointed out to me, mine is "have fun". I didn't realise I was saying it, but I love it. It sums me up more than anything else I could say.

So – what is fun for you? For that's where it starts, much like we discussed in the first chapter about success – it has to be what turns YOU on.

Check your balance

How do you spend your time – how much of it is spent doing what you want to do? Doing the stuff that makes it fun. Of course it won't always be perfectly balanced – realistically life isn't like that. But surely we should be aiming for some sort of balance.

It's time to bring back some of the things we have already discussed:

FOCUS – Make a list now of things that you love doing that can be incorporated into your daily life. It might just be having a quiet coffee on your own in a café – it doesn't have to be something huge and life-changing, just the things that make you feel good.

PRIORITISE – Don't always put yourself last. I see many people who are brilliant at organizing everything for everybody apart for themselves. You can only do one thing in one 'now', make sure some of them are for you.

DOGASHI – Shut those voices up. Especially the ones that try to make you feel guilty for having some fun and doing something for yourself!

THE THIEF OF TIME – Are you procrastinating fun? Waiting until; you have more time, more money, the kids are grown up, you retire, etc. I don't want to be morbid here, but life can be very fragile and very uncertain. Imagine putting fun off for so long that you never get the chance to enjoy it. Scary!!

Learn to love change

Whether you like it or not we live in a world of rapid change. We have to learn to love that change or it will swallow us up.

Resisting change is like standing next to an ocean, with the 'waves of change' crashing on to the beach. Well we all have simple choices in our lives. We can stand there, feet firmly planted in the sand, arms folded saying: "Well I'm not moving. I've always done it like this. Why should I change?"

But what will happen as a consequence? You will get wet feet because the waves aren't going to stop crashing in. If you still stand there ignoring the waves around your ankles, eventually you will be up to your knees and if you still don't move – YOU WILL DROWN!

We all have choices. We can get out there and ride the waves or we can stand there waiting to drown!

Change daily

If you are not great at this try incorporating some small change into your life every day, or every week if that is too daunting. I simply mean things like; eating something you wouldn't normally, taking a different route home, watching a film you wouldn't normally watch, listening to a different type of music to the usual.

These small changes will become a habit which will make the big changes easier to deal with when they happen – which they will!!

WE ALL HAVE CHOICES. WE CAN GET OUT THERE AND RIDE THE WAVES OR WE CAN STAND THERE WAITING TO DROWN!

Stress kills the fun!

Actually it kills more than the fun – it is constantly being referred to as the biggest killer of our time. The reason why is the knock on effect it has on so many life threatening conditions.

We all experience stress at different times in our life – some stress is good for you, it can energise you. However, I think we all know that the stress I am talking about isn't good for you at all.

It's not just our health though, it's how it affects our relationships, our ability to relax, wind down and have fun. Of course, we then end up using artificial methods to help, alcohol, smoking, drugs etc. Even though all the research tells us that none of these things actually reduce stress levels long-term!

None of the above sounds much like fun!

Press the pause button

Stress is cyclical so the key to controlling stress is to break the cycle.

As you start to get stressed by something, your muscles tense and chemicals are released into the blood stream – these chemicals actually make you feel more stressed, which means you tense up more, which releases more chemicals and so on.

Create a pause button for yourself that you can use to break the cycle.

I always remember my mum telling me to count to 10 – that simple piece of mothers' advice is spot on. There are many different ways of doing it. Some people use meditation techniques or simple self hypnosis.

I decided to create a physical trigger that reminded me to pause. I, like many people, put my hand to my forehead when I get stressed and so I decided to make that a reminder, my knot in a handkerchief (another piece of advice from my mum) to relax – take a breath, pause and break the cycle.

Find something that you naturally do when you are stressed and recognise it as a sign that you need to stop whenever you do it.

Breathe

The best tool I have ever used for controlling stress is to breathe! SLOWLY!!

Try breathing in for a count of between 7 and 10, whatever is comfortable.

Now hold that breath for the same count and then slowly release the breath to the same count. Keep doing this and you will start to slow your system down and give yourself the break needed to get control of stress.

The great thing about this technique is that you can do it front of people and they don't know what you are doing – it's great for controlling nerves (basically the same as stress, you have to break the cycle) or getting control in a stressful meeting etc.

Change the movies

However, the best tool for long-term control of stress and subsequently the best way to keep a balance in your life, making sure you are in the right state of mind, having fun whilst you do what you have to do to be successful, is to change those movies!

We have already discussed this in Chapter 7, but I cannot emphasise enough how important this is.

If you keep watching scary movies then be prepared to be scared all the time!

THE BEST TOOL I HAVE EVER USED FOR CONTROLLING STRESS IS TO BREATHE! SLOWLY!!

Do I want to feel like this?

As you begin to understand the control you can have if you choose to, everything you need to do to be fantastic becomes easier and so therefore is more fun.

Two questions to change your life – that's a big claim. But these two questions really can have that impact.

Next time you are not operating as you want to or how you know you should be, whether it's because you are tired, fed up, sad, de-motivated, angry, stressed or intimidated, simply ask yourself the first question.

Do I want to feel like this?

What a great question this is. The best answer would be 'NO' of course. However sometimes the answer may be yes!

I often talk about something I call the Positive Attitude Myth! Yes you read that right – myth. I think it is a myth that we have to be positive, happy, motivated at all times. However it is a myth that many books and development programmes peddle, which in my experience just ends up making people feel guilty for being normal – being human.

I prefer to talk about the 'appropriate human response'. I remember being on a programme once where the trainer used an analogy of oversleeping on the morning of an important meeting.

He suggested to us that after running around the house getting ready and rushing through the front door thinking we were just going to make it on time, to then realise we have a flat tyre.

Then he lost me – he suggested that we should be happy about this and recognise that it was meant to be. Well, I do sort of go with the 'meant to be' bit as I, like many of us, have experienced that many times. But you know what – I would swear and kick the tyre!

Which I think is actually the appropriate human response – and if I didn't do that I think I would be repressing those emotions which are just part of the balance that makes up a human being.

The key is that after kicking it, I need to re-focus on changing that tyre or finding an alternative way to get to the meeting.

Have the appropriate human response and then move past it – into another 'now' and get on with it. It's the person who keeps the negativity, anger etc., with them all day, that isn't in control.

So maybe the answer to question one is YES! Great, have your appropriate human response, but just remember to keep asking yourself question one until the answer is NO.

Then you move to question two…

What do I have to change then?

It's here where you really begin to understand responsibility. Before, you might have looked externally at this point – looked for the things that you thought were affecting you.

Let's say that a colleague annoys you at work – you might think that what you have to change is that person – but you can't.

You see, it might be hours since it happened, but you are still playing the movie over and over again in your head. It's the movie that's making you angry.

These types of things are happening all the time to all of us – the answer to question two might not always be about changing a mind movie. Maybe it's physical. Go for a walk? Or, it might simply be that you need to take more control, stop making excuses and get on with having fun and being fantastic.

There you go – two questions to change your life:

QUESTION ONE

Do I want to feel like this? Answer – NO

QUESTION TWO

What do I have to change then?

CHECK YOUR BALANCE

Are you happy with the balance in your life? Are you having fun? If so – great! If not, it's time to take action before it's too late! Nobody lays on their deathbed wishing they had spent more time at the office!! It's about balance though – maybe you are imbalanced the other way – perhaps you need to take more action! Either way, you need balance to have fun.

PRESS THE PAUSE BUTTON

Stress is a killer. Learn to relax and have some fun. Don't take things quite so seriously. Feel great about relaxing rather than guilty but most of all break the cycle. That's what stress is and when you break the stress cycle you give yourself a chance of gaining control and being able to enjoy what you are doing.

DO I WANT TO FEEL LIKE THIS?

Learn to change. Make small changes regularly so that you get used to change when the big ones come along. Take control of the movies in your head – sometimes it's those that you need to change. Ask yourself whether you want to feel this way, when you don't feel good. If the answer is no, change something!

Choose 3 goals from this chapter that you can take immediate action on:

1

2

3

10

BE FANTASTIC!

Be fantastic

Well I guess if you have got this far, I can assume that you have enjoyed 'Fantastic'. In this last chapter I want to focus on a different word though –

BE!

You see it's that little two-letter word that will actually make the difference.

You can read about Fantastic, you can talk about it, agree with it, you might even go on training programmes about it, but none of it will make any difference unless you decide to…

BE Fantastic

Let's go all the way back to chapter 2 and The Success Pyramid. It was there that I first made it clear that learning on its own won't change a thing – it's the action you take that will make sure you are Fantastic at what you do.

Remember the millionaire hairdresser?

My last three questions

Whenever I am speaking to an audience I always finish with the same three questions and as we are nearing the end of this book, let me ask you those same three questions.

Have you enjoyed it?

I hope so. Learning should always be fun!

Has it been a worthwhile read?

Have you gained something from 'Fantastic' – some insights, different tools or just the motivation to make the changes you need to?

If the answer to those first two questions is YES, then that's great and I hope you will spread the word and tell others about Fantastic – Thank you.

However, I still have one more question for you, perhaps the most important of all:

If you have enjoyed it, fantastic. If it has been worthwhile, even better. Then my final question quite simply is... What are you going to do about it?

Remember why it's a revolution – because it never stops, however fantastic you are, you have to keep it going.

It all starts with Passion – knowing where you are going and why. Then you have to get out on to the edge of the TLC and start being Creative. Delight people, inspire them, excite, surprise and WOW them. Now get on stage, Perform and be Alive Inside. Learn constantly and consistently and finally making sure you are enjoying it – having Fun!

Do the Fantastic Revolution Audit on the next page to identify where you have to put your focus, what action you have to take, what you have to learn to continue your journey to BE FANTASTIC.

THAT'S IT – BE FANTASTIC – GOOD IS NOT ENOUGH ANYMORE!! HAVE FUN!

If you want change – change something!!

Think carefully about the 7 characteristics of fantastic people and mark yourself out of 10 – with 10 being the highest. If you are unsure – go back to the relevant chapter and re-read it – you will quickly realise what mark to give yourself.

You will notice that there is no number 7 mark. Why is that? Because 7 is the safe bet – the sitting on the fence mark. It says 'I'm not too good, but not too bad either!' By taking this mark away, if you find yourself wanting to give a mark of 7, you will now have to decide whether you are more of an 8 or more a 6!!

Once you have marked yourself, now identify one piece of action you could take straight away that would start to increase your score. If you have marked 9/10 anywhere, ask yourself what you have to start doing to reach 20! Because that's what fantastic people would do!!

Now start doing it – take action – change something and feel the difference.

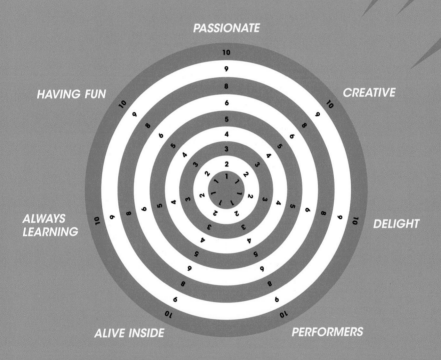

PASSIONATE

HAVING FUN

CREATIVE

ALWAYS
LEARNING

DELIGHT

ALIVE INSIDE

PERFORMERS

123

BE FANTASTIC

 PASSIONATE

 CREATIVE

 DELIGHT PEOPLE

 PERFORMERS

 ALIVE INSIDE

 ALWAYS LEARNING

 HAVING FUN

1

2

3

4

5

6

7

'Fantastic – when good is not enough' is a collaboration of two 'fantastic' companies!

Every morning Dominic Sharpe, owner of Deliverers Consultancy, walks past a building called the Fantastic Hairdresser Business Academy.

One morning he noticed a book called *The Fantastic Hairdresser* by Alan Austin-Smith in the window. It was only a few days later he saw a blog from Tom Peters, the world renowned business guru talking about the self same book. The next day he stopped and bought a copy.

As an avid learner and reader himself, he immediately knew that when he couldn't put it down and had read it from cover to cover, this was something everybody should have.

Two days later he had a meeting with Alan and his business partner Carolyn Field.

And the rest is history, with over 30 years of experience in the world of customer service, leadership and team development Carolyn and Alan joined forces with Deliverers Consultancy to create *'Fantastic – When Being Good is Not Enough!'*

With Deliverers expertise in creating unique and engaging development programmes to businesses around the world, together they have created not just an engaging and worthwhile book, but an essential understanding of what is needed in this brave new world we are all operating in today, both at work and in every area of our life.

If you have enjoyed this book, if anything here has made any sense to you whatsoever, please go to the website and join the Fantastic Revolution.

**WANT TO KNOW MORE ABOUT
WHAT ELSE WE CAN DO FOR YOU
AND YOUR BUSINESS?**

WWW.THEFANTASTICREVOLUTION.COM

*FROM BESPOKE TRAINING
PROGRAMMES, E-BOOKS, AUDIO-
BOOKS, VIDEOS AND CONFERENCE
SPEAKING TO PUBLIC SEMINARS AND
EVENTS FOR INDIVIDUALS OR
SMALLER COMPANIES.*

NOTES

Alan Austin-Smith

Alan Austin-Smith is a man on a 'fantastic' mission.

As a 16 year old, he was enticed into the exciting world of hairdressing at Vidal Sassoon in New Bond St, London. Initially attracted by the creativity on one hand and the "beautiful women, famous faces and wild parties", on the other (what teenager wouldn't be?!) he grew to love the 'business' behind the creativity. Later, inspired to join cosmetics giant L'Oréal, he became responsible for helping salons to improve their business skills.

Realising that here was a niche market, he left L'Oréal after eight years and started The Fantastic Hairdresser Company – dedicated to teaching salon owners and their team how to turn their creativity into a business.

Fascinated by successful people and what it is that makes them different, Alan has spent the last 25 years studying 'fantastic' people in all walks of life.

His first book *The Fantastic Hairdresser*, has sold over 100,000 copies. It soon started to attract the attention of people who weren't even hairdressers as the messages were transferable to anyone.

The Fantastic Boss, his second book, was voted 'a must read' by *High Life* British Airways magazine and has been used by companies around the world as an essential leadership guide.

With a return to his roots, (pardon pun) *The Fantastic Salon* became the essential guide for anyone running a business in the salon industry but now with this, his fourth book, it's time to bring the insights of 'Fantastic' to everyone!

Alan's guiding passion is 'being fantastic' – as a father, husband and friend as well as in every part of his business life and he is now in great demand around the world as an inspiring speaker who brings that passion to anyone who will listen!